BROKEN
BUT STILL USABLE

…just like me

PASTOR JOSHUA A. HALES

ISBN 979-8-88751-452-9 (paperback)
ISBN 979-8-88751-453-6 (digital)

Christian Faith Publishing
832 Park Avenue
Meadville, PA 16335
www.christianfaithpublishing.com

Printed in the United States of America

Five Star Reviews

★ ★ ★ ★ ★

I have had the pleasure of getting to know Josh over the years, and his passion for Jesus is evident when talking to him. This book was a fun read for me because, as I read these pages, I wasn't reading the story of someone who is famous or even did something extraordinary that everyone talks about. It is the story of a regular guy, like you and me, who came into contact with a radical savior who changed his life. Reading this book will make you realize two things: one, Jesus is at the center of who Josh is; and two, because of Jesus, we all have our own story to tell. I believe both mine and Josh's prayer is that you are bold enough to share it with others.

—Darrell Hornback
Chaplain
United States Air Force

I have known Josh for many years. I have watched him grow and work through the highs and lows in his life. In this book is the power of the Gospel and the fact that we must be broken. We must come to Christ for redemption. This book should give hope to those that feel hopeless and that God has given up on them. Our life, whatever we have done, still has great purpose in God's hands. We are broken but still usable for God's glory. Never give up hope!

—P. D. Hilary
Author of *Through the Eyes of an Orphan*

Kintsugi is the Japanese art of finding beauty in broken dishes. The idea is that after a dish breaks, the cracks are filled with liquid gold, actually making the dish more valuable after it has been repaired. In my opinion, Josh Hales is a "Kintsugi warrior." Having walked with Josh through some of the things he writes about in this incredible book, I can attest to the fact that these words were born out of deep brokenness. I personally saw God sustain Josh and use him in mighty ways during those difficult days of sorrow. Today, as Josh's friend and pastor, I am blessed to see how God is still using Josh (and his family) in our church on a daily basis. God is so good!

Anyone who reads this book will be both blessed and inspired by Josh's biblical teaching and transparency. As a result, I'm pretty sure there will be many more "Kintsugi warriors" born from adversity and patiently waiting to be used by an amazing God!

—David Faile
Campus Pastor
The Church At Eastmont

This book is dedicated to my family; my wife, Erin, of fifteen years; my four children, Connor (ten), Nolan (eight), Titus (six), and Makenna (two); and to my future grandchildren and greats. I love you, and I wrote this book for you. I pray that the biblical truths within these pages point (all who read them) to Jesus and help navigate life's challenges as you serve Him.

Menu

TRAILER

I found myself back at our previous church.

It was a joyous occasion, reconnecting with many familiar faces. It felt a bit like coming home. Love was in the air. My wife and I were preparing to sing for the wedding of a former volunteer student ministry leader, as she was getting ready to start the rest of her life with her new husband. We were so excited to help them both celebrate.

I was in the old restroom stall, changing into my suit. I had purchased a brand-new cell phone just days earlier. Of course, I would never have let anything happen to that wonderful, upgraded device. Why would I have needed to buy a protective phone case? Ha! As I hurried, I discarded my jeans over the stall door, launching my new phone from the back pocket like a missile straight down to destroy the tile floor. Something was broken that day, but it was not the decorative floor tile. I heard a *crash* that could only lead a person to the conclusion of "Oh, that's not good."

Have you been there? Have you felt this hurt? This heartache? Over the years that I've been in vocational ministry and have had numerous opportunities to speak to crowds of all ages, I've used this experience as an icebreaker before messages. Oftentimes, I would ask everyone to "get out their cell phones and hold them in the air." Then I would proceed to ask them to "continue holding them up only if they were cracked, broken in any way, or completely obliterated like mine." No matter the size of the audience, the percentage of people who lowered their devices would be so low that almost no one ever did. Isn't that interesting?

I still have the phone today, though this all happened several years ago. I may never get rid of it. Students and adults alike have inquired over and over again why I have not yet replaced this phone, with its web-shattered screen. My response has always been the same. "It is ***BROKEN BUT STILL USABLE...just like me.***"

I can't tell you the number of times I have been able to use this phone in an illustration that leads to a Gospel conversation. A day or two after the wedding, I was in a cell phone store purchasing a screen protector that could only be described as perfectly fitting packaging tape. When making the transaction at the counter, the twentysomething-year-old employee looked up at me in confusion and said, "Sir, you know you are supposed to put that on before you break your phone, right?"

To which I replied, "Son, I am just trying to hold all the pieces together." Wow! If that doesn't preach, I don't know what will. That worker heard about Jesus that day. AMEN.

A life lived in the service of our King is an amazing journey to enjoy. But truth be told, life is hard. Perhaps, you have learned this already, more than once, with great pain and difficulty. Maybe you are traveling the on-ramp to the next hurdle life has for you. Or possibly, you are sailing choppy waters even now as you read. This book is for you. Satan would love nothing more than to break you and convince you there is no use for you on this planet.

Our own sin struggles can speak volumes to our spirit that we are worthless. Other people can add fuel to the fire of the feelings of inadequacies, both maliciously and unintentionally. Our own declining health or that of a loved one can leave us helpless, broken. Unforeseeable circumstances and severed relationships can quickly introduce us to that rock in that hard place. It is no fun. It "feels" like a shattered phone. But our sovereign God has a purpose in it all and a plan for your life. Jesus can hold all the pieces together, I promise.

BROKEN BUT STILL USABLE is a compilation of personal testimonies as well as messages preached over my tenure as a student pastor. This is my life, my heart written down. My hope for you as a reader is to be encouraged and to know you are not alone. I desire for you to connect with my God stories and to be reminded of crucial biblical principles as they pertain to just some of Scripture's real-life accounts. At its core, this book is Gospel-driven, and I pray it points all who read it to Christ who is "the author and perfecter of our faith" (*Heb. 12:2*). Thank you for reading.

Pastor Josh

Scene 1

Prodigal

My childhood was blessed. I had good parents, a good home, and a good church.

Our family owned a mom-and-pop grocery store where I learned to work, rotating products as I stocked the shelves I could reach during my youngest years. I mastered the arts of storefront window displays and push brooming. My customer service skills were crafted as I studied at the feet of my grandma selling fresh donuts and penny candy over the ice-cream freezer. As I routinely shadowed my mother (the *world's best grocery delivery service provider* in history), I knew early on I was a people person.

I absorbed all I could from Dad's leadership, watching him place orders over the phone, handle the financials, show grace to shoplifters, and support Grandpa and my uncle as they would freely feed those who were hungry while sharing their faith over sliced meats and cheeses. I wish I could travel through time to visit myself as a child during those ham-scented car rides home to say, "Boy, you really got it good!"

Mom and Dad were not wealthy entrepreneurs, but Dad was a landlord to a few apartments and houses. They also had a side hustle, a clever street vending cotton candy business. The summer after my fifth-grade school year, our family built a new large home on a four-acre lot in the country, with three bathrooms. I thought we were rich. I never went hungry or unclothed. Our household of seven, along with our twelve chickens, three farm ducks, family dog, cat, and at any given time, a couple of birds, some fish, and hamsters, all lived in abundance.

My parents were faithful to each other and faithful to the Lord. They served at a Bible-preaching-and-teaching church where I came to trust Jesus as my Savior at the age of twelve. They were committed to our attendance there, and I was raised under the Word of God (*Prov. 22:6*). I am now so thankful, but that was not always the case.

Step Right Up

This world wants our youth. Performance-based Christianity and curbside appeal simply will not do.

Somewhere along the way, I learned to act the part—to do the right things, say the right things, and look the right way. Sadly, I was a statistic of children whose faith was in fact their parents' faith. I knew right from wrong and mostly, got it more right than wrong. I was fluent in Christianese. As we filled the back pew each Sunday, I was always dressed my best.

At about eight or nine years old, my passion and raw gift for singing began to develop. I fell in love with the applause. My hunger for performance within ministry circles only grew. Whether it was Bible trivia or memorization, an opportunity to preach a sermon during a youth service, or a Christmas drama or choir cantata, I courted the approval of man and called it spirituality.

I believe that I understood and had received salvation, but my relationship with God had not yet changed me from the inside out. I didn't serve Christ's church but rather served my own appetite for acceptance.

There is no perfect church and there are no perfect parents. I fault no one. I simply am communicating that this was my reality.

Childish Bitterness

As I grew, my dependency on approval grew as well. Especially from my father.

My adolescent years harvested legalism and unrealistic expectations of the church and its leaders, as well as my parents, but most of all, Dad. We have always been so alike and yet so different. I am an emotional person. It is one of my greatest strengths and can be an incredibly complicated weakness. Dad, on the other hand, is not emotional like me. Our personalities struggled to connect. He loved me with everything he had, but I wanted to *feel* that love in a way he possibly lacked the capacity. I fed unrighteous anger (a sin the Holy Spirit still chisels at in me today) and grew in a relationship crippling bitterness. It didn't matter if it was leading the family a cappella group in church service, a school choir or band performance, or a tennis match or wrestling meet, the applause no longer concerned me unless it was coming from the clapping of his hands. I wanted to connect, a smile, anything to meet his approval. But it felt impossible, and I was exhausted trying.

I was done. There was no way for me to fix what was "broken" in him and in us. He was never going to understand me. I was prepared to leave as soon as I could. I would find love somewhere else.

Can anyone resonate with me here, or am I the only sinner reading this? Man, do I wish I could do it all over again. I have to admit, I did think I had all the answers and that my parents were clueless. I was wrong. I now strive to honor my parents (*Eph. 6:1–3*) every opportunity and in any way I can, though obeying them (*Col.*

3:20) as a teen was just not a goal. Had I figured this out earlier in life, I could have saved myself a lot of suffering. Stubborn immaturity causes us to learn things the hard way. So I left.

5

Terrible Twenties

All that I needed was available to me in Christ, but I was not looking to Him for it.

It seems each decade of my life has had its own lessons to be learned. If my childhood years were when I came to faith and my teenage years were when I grew to fully understand my faith, my twenties were certainly when that faith was tested.

I left home with nowhere to go, no way to earn a living, no credit, no real plan, and a giant chip on my shoulder. One of my brothers who owned and operated a landscaping business not only provided temp work for me on a number of occasions but also cosigned an apartment as well as a car at one time. It was my sin that put me in need, and I was undeserving of his generosity. I am certain I took him for granted as I so often did my parents. I needed to repent and go back home, but unfortunately, pride kept me down a destructive path.

I eventually was engaged to be married to someone I had no business being in a relationship with. Not as a Christian. I ignored all warning signs and red flags, happy to turn my back on family, friends, and faith, running full speed away from all I knew to be truth. I was "doubling down" on us and "putting all my eggs in her basket." Until the relationship broke, then I broke. I was truly alone, and it was all my fault.

During this time, I was introduced to the world of alcohol. It got a hold of me hard and fast. The depression was bad but even worse was the self-medicating. I knew I had a problem, but I didn't care. I was mad—mad at my father and mad at my family. I was angry with the church and with my ex-fiancé. I was enraged all the time, at perfect strangers, at life, and at God. My "temperature" was always high, and the only thing that could bring it down was the alcohol that just reminded me how incredibly sad I was as well. It was a vicious cycle.

At one point, I was working three jobs to support my habit. I was addicted. I was an alcoholic. My kitchen and fridge were full, but I had no food. I was terminated from my third-shift employment as a cargo handler on the runway of an airport, sent home in a taxi, intoxicated. I was a loser. When you are on your couch, drinking by yourself at 3:00 a.m. every morning, you are a loser. I remember literally shaking my finger in the air at God and screaming, "I don't need you, and I don't want you. I'm going to live for me now!" That is dangerous. I was not sober for the good part of a year.

I didn't care if I woke up the next day, so why would I care what I did while I was awake? I was drowning in my sin and reached a new level of selfishness. I decided to drink myself to death. The fact that I authored this book is proof I was not successful. I was ready to give up, but God did not give up on me.

Late in the morning, I regained consciousness, lying in my own bloody vomit, halfway hanging over the top of the stairway, unable to stand. This was not a rare occasion for me, but this time was different. I was hurt badly. I needed medical attention. I clearly had alcohol poisoning and belonged in a hospital. All the blood vessels in both my eyes were busted, most likely from the violent vomiting across every space in the apartment that I could not remember. When I finally pulled myself up after crawling to the bathroom sink, I didn't recognize the person in the mirror. I broke. I was broken. I hit rock bottom, and it was at that moment I learned just how solid the rock (Jesus) is (*Ps. 18:2*).

I had not talked to the Lord in what seemed like forever, but in quivering desperation, I spoke out loud, "God, I need you. If you will save me from myself, I will give you my life."

Open Arms

I didn't hear God audibly that day, but He spoke to me like I had never experienced.

"Josh, I have never left you (*Heb. 13:5*). I have always been right here, Son. I have been protecting you, waiting for you to call on my name. I have a plan for you. You're going to live for me now!"

At that moment, I did not know what He meant. It didn't matter. I repented. I turned away from my sin, and I ran toward Christ. I reached for my Bible, something I had not done in ages.

I can't express the frequency of times I should have been wrapped around a telephone pole, never to receive even a single DUI. How foolish are recreational relationships under the influence and the many vague, foggy memories that perhaps point to experiences without recalling faces or even clarity of details? I should not be alive. The Lord would have been right to wipe me out of existence. I was actively detouring people away from Him. But He is a good Father, with unending, undeserving, grace, mercy, and love.

My 3:00 a.m. couch visits were still happening, with the Bible in my shaking hand, as my body repeatedly told me I needed a drink. I was communing with the Holy Spirit as I sobered, and a change was taking place in my heart. There was no applause, and I was on a new path, convicted to perform for an audience of ONE.

Right Place At The Right Time

Outside of the Gospels, the book of Ecclesiastes is the one book of the Bible that has had the greatest impact on my life.

I had never really studied Ecclesiastes before. It's a short read. Just twelve chapters. Depraved of hope it would seem. We are confident King Solomon authored this wisdom literature book that clearly communicates (to his son) that life is meaningless, "chasing after the wind." Or does it communicate something much more profound?

Let's first remember that Solomon was the son of King David, "a man after God's own heart" (*1 Sam. 13:14*). His very existence came about through David's unfortunate sin, an immoral polygamous marriage to Bathsheba, who was previously married to Uriah. David essentially murdered Uriah, placing the soldier in the front of battle after a deceptive affair with his wife. Make no mistake about it, throughout the pages of Scripture, we see within ancestry lines that sin breeds more sin from generation to generation. What we do as parents directly affects our kids.

Solomon took the throne of Israel incredibly young. He easily could have come up through many of the church ministries I've had the privilege of pastoring. God used young people in the Old Testament, and He still uses them today. We see in *1 Kings 3*, when he was near the age of twenty, the Lord spoke to Solomon in a dream offering anything he would ask of Him. He asked for wisdom. Here is what happened.

It pleased the Lord that Solomon had asked
this. And God said to him, "Because you have asked

> *this, and have not asked for yourself long life or riches or the life of your enemies, but have asked for yourself understanding to discern what is right, behold, I now do according to your word. Behold, I give you a wise and discerning mind, so that none like you has been before you and none like you shall arise after you. I give you also what you have not asked, both riches and honor, so that no other king shall compare with you, all your days. And if you will walk in my ways, keeping my statutes and my commandments, as your father David walked, then I will lengthen your days." (1 Kings 3:10–14 ESV)*

Solomon received wisdom from the creator of the universe. Apart from Jesus (God in flesh), no one has yet or ever will come close to his level of wisdom gifted him. In direct response to his already wise and unselfish request, God blessed Solomon with wealth that Amazon's Jeff Bezos could only hope for. He also received a covenant of long life if he would commit to following the Lord in obedience. This wise preacher is who penned Ecclesiastes.

Although King Solomon was enriched with Heavenly wisdom, he was kind of an idiot. And as I studied this book anew, I found myself relating to this man. What I heard him saying to his son, to the people of that day, and to me in that Holy Spirit life-changing moment was, "Learn from my mistakes so that you do not need to learn from yours." I was drawing from his great wisdom, what he had learned perhaps too late in his life. For me though, this was an opportunity for a fresh start.

Solomon pursued happiness in all this world and life has to offer, but it kept him empty and unsatisfied. Let's read about it in *Ecclesiastes 2*.

> *I said in my heart, "Come now, I will test you with pleasure; enjoy yourself." But behold, this also was vanity. I said of laughter, "It is mad," and of pleasure, "What use is it?" I searched with my heart*

how to cheer my body with wine—my heart still guiding me with wisdom—and how to lay hold on folly, till I might see what was good for the children of man to do under heaven during the few days of their life. I made great works. I built houses and planted vineyards for myself. I made myself gardens and parks, and planted in them all kinds of fruit trees. I made myself pools from which to water the forest of growing trees. I bought male and female slaves, and had slaves who were born in my house. I had also great possessions of herds and flocks, more than any who had been before me in Jerusalem. I also gathered for myself silver and gold and the treasure of kings and provinces. I got singers, both men and women, and many concubines, the delight of the sons of man.

So I became great and surpassed all who were before me in Jerusalem. Also my wisdom remained with me. And whatever my eyes desired I did not keep from them. I kept my heart from no pleasure, for my heart found pleasure in all my toil, and this was my reward for all my toil. Then I considered all that my hands had done and the toil I had expended in doing it, and behold, all was vanity and a striving after wind, and there was nothing to be gained under the sun. (Ecc. 2:1–11 ESV)

Solomon tried to experience enjoyment in pleasurable things—in alcohol, in accomplishments, in mass amounts of stuff, in sheer wealth, in power and position, in entertainment, and in women. He had hundreds of concubines, "wives" on the side. I would say it is fair to call him an immoral man. Culturally acceptable at that time but unbiblical. He was outside of God's design and plan for marriage (*Gen. 2:24*).

Did you catch the highlighted part above in *verse 10*? He denied himself nothing. If he wanted it, he got it. It is a safe bet none of my readers could do the same. Yet, his thirst was never quenched. His life's search constantly left him broken. The reason for this is that we were never put on this earth for any of these things. If we run after these things to fulfill our lives, we are worshiping the created—the sin of idolatry. Our FULL satisfaction must be found in Jesus Christ alone. I will talk more about that later in Scene 3 in this book.

The Meaning Of Life

It has been said that humanity exists for three reasons:

    (1) To glorify God.
    (2) To glorify God.
    (3) To glorify God.

That is why you are here. That is your purpose. That is God's will for you. Solomon's conclusion is found in what I still consider to be my life verse.

> *The end of the matter; all has been heard.*
> *Fear God and keep his commandments, for this is*
> *the whole duty of man. (Ecc. 12:13 ESV)*

Let's break this down. The preacher is not telling us to go hide in the corner shaking because of what God might do to us. To fear God is to revere God—to place Him in a position of reverence. He is first. He is most. Nothing comes before or above Him. He is number one. Even the most committed disciple has room for improvement in this area of their life, and certainly, I do as well. But that night as I read, Christ's position in my life changed, and I have not looked back since.

God's rightful positioning in our hearts brings us to the desire to live our lives in obedience, as an act of worship, to the one who is worthy of our devotion and love. When our children were very young, we would make it a practice to recite the same mission statement before bed each night, "Jesus died for me, so I will live for Him." Not many things bring more joy than to hear the precious voices of your own preschoolers speak such words.

To fear God and to keep His commandments is our duty. When our lives no longer are about us but become about Him and reaching others with the good news of the Gospel, our dependencies shift. Selflessness replaces the selfish. Repentance and forgiveness remove bitterness and hatred. And the seeking of gratification becomes a mission to serve the King of Kings. We wear out our knees with our faces to the ground and our hearts yearning for more of Jesus, which in turn brings about less of ourselves (*John 3:30*).

True Repentance Produces Change

Grab a pen and paper. Jesus is about to speak.

> *But when the Pharisees heard that he had silenced the Sadducees, they gathered together. And one of them, a lawyer, asked him a question to test him. "Teacher, which is the great commandment in the Law?" And he said to him, "You shall love the Lord your God with all your heart and with all your soul and with all your mind. This is the great and first commandment. And a second is like it: You shall love your neighbor as yourself. On these two commandments depend all the Law and the Prophets." (Matt. 22:34–40 ESV)*

We see here Jesus being directly asked which is the greatest of God's commandments. It was such a fantastic question that the motive behind asking it was insignificant. Anyone who claims the name of the Lord should pay extra attention to a text like this. It should be something to build your life and ministry around. This passage feels a bit like the professor giving his class the answers before the big test.

As the Holy Spirit got a hold of me, I genuinely began to love Jesus. I love Him, because He first loved me (*1 John 4:19*). He has not stopped changing my heart. It's been over nineteen years since my last drink. Praise God! The Holy Spirit continues to move and work in my life. I did not know then the exciting adventure ahead, but (by God's grace) never again was I to take a step without the leading of His Spirit. The Lord rescued my mind and renewed it (*Rom. 12:2*), and now there was a job to do. It was time to get to work.

Deep within me, a passion for the Gospel exploded. I had overwhelming compassion for others and a new energy to serve them. I was finally *seeing* lost people, and my heart was pumping evangelistically. This was not Josh. This was Jesus in me. But it was only the beginning.

I would like to say the change in me was overnight, but it was not a Dr. Jekyll/Mr. Hyde scenario. It was a process over the next several months and even years. It involved different circumstances with dozens of people. The journey was incredible, though there were certainly potholes along the way. The Bible had become a lifeline, and my time spent with the Lord was personal and intimate. I needed to get back to church, and I wanted to be busy doing Kingdom work. First though, in biblical obedience, I had to get things right with my family. I had to get things right with Dad.

A Lot To Prove

I lived just a couple hours away. So attending service at my home church was doable.

Each Sunday morning, I would wake extra early to be sure my travels would not delay being on time. I talked to God a lot in the car. I remember the first time I showed up. The worship service took place like normal. We sang. We prayed. We read from Scripture. The message was delivered, and then we all went home. My commute was the longest, I am sure. A lot of eyes were on me. I sat near the family but never felt more distant. This went on for weeks, and I felt sad and empty each time. But I knew God was asking me to do it.

After a couple of months, I was invited home for Sunday lunch. Nothing tastes quite like Mom's cooking. I was so happy to be home again. I grew up in a large family, where we talked and laughed, but meals were really never quiet. This one was. The conversations surrounding that table were of my repentance and their forgiveness. We prayed together, and there were lots of tears and hugs. The Lord was glorified.

I had abandoned all of them and was far from God. I knew that they knew letting me back into their lives was a risk and that they would be watching in the days ahead for real change in my life. Understandable. But I no longer would care what anyone else thought of me more than I cared what Jesus thought of me. It was Him and me from now on. I was living my life for Christ.

The Big Move

Our plans are never as big as God's plans (*Jer. 29:11*). His timing is always perfect, and He is always on time.

Fast forward some real progress in reconciliation. I was still growing, and Dad (and the family) and I were doing very well. When I allowed the Holy Spirit to change me, it birthed the opportunity to change us. God was fixing what I had broken. In just a few short years, Dad would honor me and stand beside me as my best man in my wedding. No one else was qualified for the title. I don't think we have ever been closer than we are today.

A number of things factored into my plans to leave Northern Ohio and start life fresh in Western Pennsylvania. I knew then why I was moving, but I know only now what God was doing behind the scenes. Dad was not sure about my decision. We were strong, and I think his fatherly instincts wanted to protect me from repeating any past mistakes. I can't blame him. But I was supposed to go. Crossing state lines meant I was close enough to visit family often, but a new chapter in life was about to be written. Only this time, Jesus was the "captain of my ship."

I moved into my new apartment and took some time to get settled and transfer work. During a Wednesday night Bible study and prayer service, I walked into the sanctuary of a beautiful church in the city, then in my early twenties. I was wearing a T-shirt, shorts, and sandals. It seemed everyone in attendance was either a senior citizen or just shy of it. The men in the room were all wearing ties, if not a full suit. I stuck out like a sore thumb.

That church knew how to love people. So much so, that the thought of even attending another ministry was not an option for me. They became my surrogate family, and I was "home." That first Wednesday evening, I met the lead pastor, and we talked in his office for hours, late into the night. He made himself available. He genuinely cared about me and my relationship with the Lord, even though we had just met. I shared with him much of what I have already written here, what brought me to the church, and how God was moving in my life.

Our first encounter led to some amazing opportunities to actively love God and love others. The church was part of a local AM radio program, as well as a school. The lead pastor was also an executive director of a nearby camp. I served often alongside the worship pastor, who became a close friend and was also a part of my wedding party. In addition to the worship ministry, I helped with the student ministry some and got really plugged in at the camp—music, counseling, washing dishes, and scrubbing toilets. Anywhere I could serve others. My wife and I were both on staff there before we were married. What I quickly discovered was that there is no better Christ-like character building tool than to serve. So my sleeves were rolled up looking for the next opportunity to point someone to Jesus.

I was a member of that church, and for three and a half years, I was mentored and discipled by the lead pastor. His loyalty to me even today is a gift from God I do not deserve and is a rare find. He is one of my best friends, still always available for counsel and prayer. We stay close, and we are partners in ministry, even from a distance. (*This book's pages are seasoned with his illustrations, principles, and teaching on the Christian life.*) He officiated our wedding, and it was at that church, with those people, my wife and I committed our lives to one another.

God was preparing me to be a pastor. I was learning hands-on what it meant to love people. At that time, I still did not know God's call on my life to local church ministry. My path was so nontraditional. In many ways, because of my past, I was "behind the eight-ball" in financial stability and preparation. But I truly believe the Lord does not call the equipped. He equips the called. If you would have asked me during the worst of my drinking if I thought God would ever call me to be a pastor, I would have laughed in your face. God couldn't use me. I was a mess. I was too broken.

During those years of growth and mining out giftedness, the Lord opened doors for me to sing mini concerts and preach, filling pulpits in a number of small Western Pennsylvania churches. I am nowhere close to where I want to be as a communicator of the Word of God, but I am so much further today than I was back then. I was bad. But God used it. He used it to bless those saints, to make the name of Jesus famous, and to prepare me for what was to come. It was during that time the Holy Spirit began to stir my heart, and I felt the call to pastoral ministry.

Straight Shooting

I want to speak directly now to four categories of people possibly reading this book, who *have* trusted Jesus as Savior and Lord. This is completely my experiential perspective, from my heart to yours.

**The parent with the broken relationship with their adult child.
The adult child with the broken relationship with their parent.
The brokenhearted.
The one broken by alcohol.**

Mom and Dad, you have done a great job. There is no such thing as a perfect parent. Your kids will eventually figure out that you actually knew a thing or two and that parenting is quite challenging, and perfection is impossible. We hope and pray we have done enough good that our kids will be even better parents than us. If we are all successful in "passing down the torch," our great, great grandchildren will be excellent parents someday. We love the best we know how, and we realize they were never ours to begin with. God loves them more than we ever could. We pour into them His Word, and we hope that what is taught is (more importantly) caught.

If there is sin in their lives, it may feel like it is your failure, but it's not. It is their sin. Be willing to forgive as soon as true repentance takes place. Repent yourself if you have sinned against them. No matter the past, live holy now. Trust me, they want to fix what is broken between you, even if they do not know how. God is in the business of reconciliation and restoration.

In the meantime, callous your knees, lifting them up in prayer continually (*1 Thess. 5:17*). Do not stop. They are His. He is sovereign and much more capable than we are to change their hearts. Your prayers are not a last resort. They are the most important thing you can be doing. I am a living testimony of how BIG God is and what He can do in the life of your child.

Son, **daughter**, your parents love you. They always have. They've wanted the best for you, even if that meant sacrificing your happiness temporarily. Their discipline was necessary and obedience to the Lord. They have exhausted themselves by raising you. They've provided for you everything since day one so that you could experience the best life possible. Believe me when I say, they know sacrificial love.

Never expect of them more than what is reasonable. They are broken in their sin, just like you. Think often of the blessings they have provided and the happy memories you have undoubtedly had with them over the years. Hold tight to the life lessons they taught you and the truth they raised you under. God used them so that you would know Him.

Repent of your sin. Do not justify it or make excuses. Don't negotiate with your own spirit on this. Make it right, and if necessary, forgive them without hesitation. Repent to the Lord, repent to them. Do not try to save face. Don't care what people think. You have only the rest of your lives together. Do not wait another moment. Honor them, and live for Jesus.

Your heart is broken. It is weighed down by your current circumstances. The relationship that you have invested so much in is now over, and you just don't understand. Or perhaps, it is the ongoing relationship that is most difficult, and you wish for an escape. Losing someone to death is numbing, whether it is unexpected or you have had time to process it. A friendship. A marriage. A business partner. A family member. You know it is your fault. Maybe you have done nothing wrong, and someone else is causing the pain. The dynamite has been set strategically across the bridge, awaiting complete demolition. Your sorrow is deep, and you just don't want to feel this way anymore.

Jesus loves you. You are not alone. He knows exactly how you feel. His heart is broken each time we rebel against Him. He laid down His life for you because of your sin (*Rom. 5:8*). He wants to mend your heart. Fall into His arms. They are big enough. His hands are able to heal, though we have scarred them. All that matters right now is Christ. He wants you, and you need Him.

Nothing and no one else is going to replace the hurt. Mourn the loss. Get into God's Word and on your knees nonstop. Jesus will be there waiting to speak into your life. Surround yourself with God's people who also love you and serve others as often as possible. You will not feel this brokenness when you are leading someone else to the Lord. God will make you whole again.

Alcohol has nothing to offer you. NOTHING! It is a poison that slowly destroys your body on a cellular level. It steals control of your ability to reason and process thought. Scripture is littered with warnings against it. Today's alcoholic beverage, of any kind, is designed to intoxicate. Drunkenness is sin (*Eph. 5:18*). The behavioral changes it brings oftentimes compounds that sin. It is addictive. It is dangerous. It ruins lives. It kills. And Satan is a big fan of it.

If you have been broken by alcohol, and it already has a hold of you, RUN. Surrender this to the Lord. Get away from its influence at all costs. Dump what you have down the drain. Spend your time with godly people who do not consume. Place accountability in your life, including with your purchases. Get help. Biblical counsel. Licensed therapy. Medical assistance. Whatever it takes, but RUN. Nothing is impossible for God.

SCENE 2

Going To The Chapel

I should CREDIT a major source that combined with my original thoughts and teaching over the years on the topics here in Scene 2, makes up much of the ingredient list for this "spiritual pot of gumbo."
https://www.desiringgod.org/messages/sex-and-the-single-man

I want to give you full permission not to commit to my *positions*, *opinions*, or *personal thoughts* on this next section of the book. Much of what is written here is *me*, but I believe it is supported by biblical principles. Please, hold on to the truth of the absolutes and nonnegotiables of Scripture. We must commit to the definitives of God's Word.

So what is this all about? What could I possibly discuss here that would lead me to feel the need for such a disclaimer? Is there anything that pertains to the Christian life that could cause believers to lean toward multiple different camps? YUP!

We are going to discuss *Dating And Purity As It Relates To God's Design And Plan For Marriage*. And *wow*, has my heart changed on so much of these topics over the years, since as early as my own adolescence.

Whether you are a student or an adult, single or married, with or without children, I believe there is something here for you. Please pray (with me) that as you read on, the Lord may reveal His truth to you. It is my challenge that we would think differently than the world on this and that we would not be so quick to accept the popular school of thought. This is too important to not filter through Christ.

Wearing a "pastor's hat" and communicating from a father's heart, I invite you to imagine you are a student in one of my past ministries, sitting under this teaching. I will share many of the experiences during this series, but I want you to "place yourself there" and participate as you read. In your mind, provide your own heart's answers to questions presented to the group. Be willing to consider the possibility of thinking differently on this if you come to the conclusion that Jesus does. You will be given the opportunity to respond to what the Holy Spirit is telling you, and I hope you will.

Okay. Buckle yourselves in. Here we go.

Biblical Courtship

What does the Bible say about dating?

I ask this question to single young adults, college students, but mostly to teenage audiences. Without fail, it is immediately followed by a long pause of silent thinking, just before the same correct answer is given each time. NOTHING.

The Bible has nothing to say on our culture of dating. But dating exists. We can't deny that. So how do we navigate this biblically?

As a Christian, what is the purpose of dating?

When I ask this question, it always conceives the spiritual (yet correct) answer. MARRIAGE. Let's be perfectly clear. Whenever the Bible speaks on an appropriate intimate male-female relationship within God's design and will, it is *always* referring to marriage (i.e., *Num. 30:3–16*). That alone goes against the grain of current culture.

Now, imagine a room filled with a large group of coed teenagers, ranging from middle school to almost graduating seniors. Many of these students have already participated in dating relationships, and unfortunately, many of those have also experienced the physical and/or emotional equivalent of divorce. Some, multiple times. This is brokenness God does not want for those who are married, let alone a youth finding their way through years of breakup practice.

The church has got to talk about this stuff. Pastors, we must have these conversations looking through the lens of the Bible. The world will not hesitate to make available their own lesson plans. When I think of my growing children, it swells my heart even more, and I know I have a job to do as a father that I cannot fail. I don't have all the answers. But I have a number of them, now at forty-one, that I desperately needed at fourteen.

What is the perfect age to start dating?

As you can imagine, the room would now explode with a crazy variety of answers and opinions. "Thirteen, because then you are a teenager."

"*Are you kidding me?*"

"Sixteen, because you can get your license and actually go somewhere."

"*Logical.*"

"Eighteen, because then you are an adult."

"*Who says?*"

"When my dad says I can."

"*That's actually a great answer, by the way.*"

"It doesn't matter how old you are, as long as you are mature enough."

"*Wow! Really?*"

"In college, because then you are more likely to marry that person."

"*Interesting.*"

"Eleven, because I had my first relationship when I was ten, but I wasn't quite ready yet."

"*That one hurts.*"

It is obvious that we will not all agree on a "perfect" age to start dating. So I ask that we come together as a group in consensual agreement. This usually unifies us to a practical middle ground. Every group's decision is different. For our purposes now, let's say the group landed at seventeen years old. We have decided that seventeen is the perfect age to start dating.

What is the perfect age to get married?

Okay, here we go again.

"Nineteen, because you are legally an adult and have a little life experience."

"*Very little.*"

"Any time you are in college, because you are then on your own."

"*Never mind you don't have two nickels to rub together, and your parents are paying for everything.*"

"When you graduate college, because then you have got that behind you, and you are ready for marriage."

"*Okay. Twenty-one/twenty-two at the earliest of a four-year degree.*"

"When my dad says I can."

"*She is trying to be funny, but it is still a great answer.*"

"Not until you are thirty, because then you know you are really ready and mature enough."

"*Not always the case.*"

Again, a lot of different answers and thoughts here. I may offer my suggestions. My wife was twenty-three when we were married. I was twenty-five. Let's say the middle ground agreement for us, here and now, is twenty-four. We have decided as a group that twenty-four is the "perfect" age to get married.

I quiet the excitement. Using our agreed-upon answers as just one example of many others similar, I may refer to a young married couple in the room on the leadership team. When my wife and I were younger and early in ministry, I might have used us to illustrate this next point.

"As a group, you have unanimously decided that it is totally appropriate for a Christian to participate in a seven-year dating relationship prior to marriage. There is no question that at the end of that time, you will have experienced a level of intimacy with that other person (in seven years) that far surpasses that of Erin and myself (young and newer in ministry), and WE'RE MARRIED." Or pointing to the other young married couple in the room, on the team, "they have still NOT YET EXPERIENCED A SEVEN-YEAR RELATIONSHIP."

I propose at least one of two outcomes will happen given this scenario. (1) A MORAL FAILURE. Intimacy only grows over time. I could not have stayed in a seven-year dating relationship with Erin and remained pure. No way. (2) A BREAKUP. There will be broken hearts here. The pain will be much worse, depending on the level of physical intimate liberties taken between the couple. Unfortunately, those in the room that have dated in the past or are currently dating someone have likely already experienced a breakup. Only strengthening my proposal.

Who would sign up for this?

(Silence)

It is at this point in the dialogue that I want to suggest a different way of thinking. I remind the group that no relationship of any kind should be void of Jesus smack-dab in the middle of things. I may ask all the gentlemen to stand. Speaking directly to them, I will refer to the ladies and say, "All of them should be FRIENDS with all of you." I will then repeat the idea to the ladies about the guys.

A great illustration to drive this home is that of a buffet. The room will fill with laughter as Tommy becomes mashed potatoes, and Tina is a giant spoonful of corn. You would not load your plate up with a mountain of freshly baked rolls and nothing else. It is healthy for you when you get "a little of everything" and your focus is on good godly friendships. You may get sick if all you do is fill up on only your favorite dessert.

Another wonderful object lesson is that of two roses. One rose is just a bud, closed tight. It has the potential to become something beautiful. I talk about dating too early, in our own strength, outside of God's will, doing things our way. I slowly force the unready flower petals open as they fall to the ground, one by one, until I am standing there with an ugly stem. A broken, dead flower. Then I pull out a second rose, healthy and fully blossomed, gorgeous. With proper watering and sunlight, nutritious soil and care, in the right timing, it has realized its potential. The rose had taken the course the caregiver knew was needed, and was now alive, strong, and beautiful. I then hand it to my bride.

I usually talk from the perspective of the guy in the relationship, because I am one, and I believe he should be providing spiritual leadership even before marriage. Without making anyone feel too targeted (There are always "couples" in the room.), I suggest that a relationship title (boyfriend/girlfriend) or physical intimacy (even something as "innocent" as an arm around the other or holding hands) communicates *loudly* to the other person (and those around) that "YOU ARE MINE." But she is not yours. She is God's. And she is her dad's. And you should protect her heart, as well as your own (*Prov. 4:23*).

I then hold up my left hand, pointing to my wedding ring. I usually say something like this, "The only people in this room that should be staking claim on another person or participating in *any* type of physical relationship are the people who have one of these." Referring to my wife, I will then say, "God and her mom and dad gave her to me. She is mine, and I am hers. We are licensed. We get to chase each other around the house." (*Laughter.*) She and I are now *not* a part of the buffet but rather full-course meals, ordered and purchased, and no longer on the menu. Our marriage is God's beautiful rose that He continues to care for and grow. His way is always the best way.

Might I suggest my practical advice?

If you cannot see yourself married in a year, do not date. If you are unable to provide a home for a family or not emotionally ready for a lifelong commitment, *wait* and enjoy many friendships with the opposite sex while seeking God. Pray daily for your future spouse. Remain pure. If you enter into a dating relationship knowing that it is not yet God's timing and you are not ready for marriage, then the only alternative is that you are doing it for recreational purposes. This is *self*-motivated and not of Christ (*Phil. 2:3*).

On the flip side, when you are ready, it is not best for you to prepare for marriage alone. Allow older, spiritually mature, married couples in the church to come alongside you. Have your pastors' counsel and involvement in the relationship. Your parents should be mentoring you as well as a part of the decision process. Accountability in purity is crucial, perhaps even more so when even engaged. When all are in agreement (including you and your prospective future mate) that the two of you should be married, there should be no confusion. God will bring this process to complete clarity.

I am not suggesting the need to return to the arranged marriages of biblical times. I also do not believe that we are on some scavenger hunt, searching for "the *one* for me." God allows us the awesome privilege and freedom to choose a life partner. Choose wisely. We should be seeking after Him, young or old, single or married, before and after that choice, and by God's grace, becoming more and more His *one* for her (or him).

Pure Purity

God's call to purity in our lives is no small thing, especially when inundated with immoral images and headlines that fight for our attention everywhere we go. From Hollywood to social media, we cannot escape it. Again, Jesus must be our full satisfaction, and Holy Spirit dependency is a necessity. Placing accountability in our lives is not weak, it is wise.

We know His design and plan for sexual intimacy is good and should exist only within marriage. The Bible is clear that when we step out of these parameters, we pervert God's creation. There are things we *need* to survive. Oxygen. Water. Food (though most of us don't handle this one properly either). Sex is not on the list. It is part of God's design and plan for marriage, a gift we get to enjoy with our spouse till death do us part.

Believe it or not, abstinence prior to marriage is just a piece of the bigger picture of purity. It is an issue of the heart even more than a list of the dos and don'ts of physical intimacy.

"Do not answer this out loud, but how many of you in this room have already taken part in any level ('big or small') of a physical relationship with a member of the opposite sex? If I were to do with another woman, not my wife, what you have already done (or are currently justifying) with the one you are dating, would you classify my actions as adultery? Could there be a double standard here? Be honest, are you doing what you are doing to glorify God? Have you prayed about it? Is it motivated by sacrificial love or by self-gratification?"

Statistically, most, if not all of these students, will be married someday. I suppose they could marry their current dating partner, but they are not married yet and have no way of knowing for sure if they would eventually be married. From the male perspective, the Bible tells us that we are to relate to all females, younger and older, as if they are our sister and/or mother (*1 Tim. 5:2*). (The same for the ladies, regarding the guys, their brother and/or father.) There is only one woman that alone categorizes uniquely from these other familial relationships, where physical intimacy and sexual encounters are appropriate, designed for, and expected—the wife.

The last thing anyone wants is to walk down the aisle on their wedding day carrying a long list of impure past relationships that stole pieces of their heart and mind away from the life partner God intended them to be whole for. My wife deserves every kiss, hand hold, hug, romantic stare, every intimate conversation, and every sexual thought. They belong to her.

How about your thought life?

"Before or after marriage, our eyes, our thoughts, and our hearts should all be motivated by our love and our worship of Christ. Our spouse is the only person He intended to receive our sexual emotions, conversations, imagination, and enticements. I need to have eyes for only Erin. And even in all of this, my heart should be to glorify God and to serve my wife."

Pro No Pornography

It is God's will that you should be sanctified: that you should avoid sexual immorality; that each of you should learn to control your own body in a way that is holy and honorable. (1 Thes. 4:3–4 NIV)

Pornography is evil. It is demonic, and it is not an option for the Christian. It is readily available to young men, dads, and pastors and is destroying lives, marriages, and ministries. More and more, it is an issue for women as well. It is just as addictive as any drug. Jesus clearly commands lust is sin.

> *"You have heard that it was said, 'You shall not commit adultery.' But I say to you that everyone who looks at a woman with lustful intent has already committed adultery with her in his heart."*
> *(Matt. 5:27–28 ESV)*

This is a battle that will not just go away, and to which, surrender can never happen.

I remember as a young student pastor, the first time a father came to me for counsel, heartbroken over learning of his teenage son's secret struggle with pornography. Then, I had no children of my own, and I still do not know now what it is to have a teenage son yet. I worked with teenagers, and I was one. What could I possibly have to offer this older man who in many ways was much more qualified to counsel me?

Back then, device options were still pretty limited to desktops and maybe laptops. Today, the internet is available at any time, in any location, and can be easily put away in one's pocket. But I remember asking him this question first, "Where is your son's computer?"

To which he replied, "In his bedroom." In my immature practical common sense, I wanted to scream at the top of my lungs, "DUH!" Don't worry, I didn't.

Even more comical, my oldest grade school son recently asked me, "When am I allowed to have my own phone?"

I replied, "When your wife lets you."

I am not casting judgment on anyone else's parenting decisions when it comes to technology. But when my *second grader* tells me that everyone else in his class at school has their own personal cell phone, it wrenches my heart.

I realize my children will never know a world without the internet. They may never fully understand a landline. It will not be long until my ten-year-old son knows more about computers than me, if he doesn't already. Much of their education involves screens, whether I like it or not. But I do have the choice to be a dad heavily involved in their lives—a dad leading important conversations and a dad living a pure example.

Feeling uncomfortable and being "not good at talking about this stuff" is not going to cut it. Allowing someone else to be the primary source of God's Word being poured into my children and to spiritually lead them through these very real dangers is just unacceptable. God gave me that responsibility as their father.

Students, young men, you have to have these conversations with your dads. Satan wins in this area of our lives when we are quiet and alone in the battle. SPEAK UP. NEVER STOP FIGHTING. Fathers, protect your sons, at all costs. Whatever it takes. Live holy so that you can walk with them pure.

We need other godly men truly keeping us accountable in this area of our lives. Older men. Men our age. The conversations we do not want to have need to happen often and honestly. Assemble a spiritual purity squad, and report regularly. Do not believe the lie that you can (or that you will) have any success in this alone.

There are many creative and practical things we can do to guard ourselves and our homes. Passwords (allowing access) trusted only to our spouses. Parental controls. Internet accountability/firewall software. The list goes on and on. Unfortunately, we live in a world where computers, devices, technology, and mostly the internet, are unavoidable. These can be great tools to perform our jobs, entertain our families, and even serve the Kingdom of God. But at the push of a button, we can see and experience *anything*, without restriction. We need to be self-aware of those restrictions we *should* place in our own lives, within our accountability, for the purpose of honoring the Lord.

Here are two ministry resources I have highly recommended for years. The *Every Man's Battle* book series can be found at www.newlife.com and has materials for guys and ladies of any age and stage in life. Along with New Life Ministries, I would also recommend the internet accountability of www.covenanteyes.com in every arsenal as God's people continue to fight in the battle against pornography.

Modest Modesty

Ladies, God made you beautiful, and He made men notice. Both of these truths are a good thing.

It has never been your responsibility to be our self-control. *We* are accountable for our actions before the Lord. But *you* can help your brothers tremendously. Commit to no flirtatious behavior. Do not fish for responses from the guys in order to feel desirable. Do not allow inappropriate sexual conversations with anyone who is not your husband. From the bottom of my daddy heart, I am begging, do not let any boy touch you.

Someday, a young man is going to ask to date my daughter. I hope he loves the Lord. I will have a simple rule. "You date my daughter, you don't touch her. You touch my daughter, you don't date her." She may kick and scream all the way there, but on her wedding day, I can already hear her whispering in my ear, "Thank you, Daddy." She belongs to me until I give her to you. It is my job to get her down the aisle pure. By the way, this will apply to my sons as well, concerning future other daddies' little girls.

There have been so many cultural shifts over time when it comes to fashion. I am sure there have been just as many guidelines established by an innumerable amount of organizations when it comes to wardrobe. Let me say this, Christian or secular, no matter the establishment or event, in humility and in Christ's love, abide by the dress code set in place. You will *never* disappoint God by being *too moral, too pure,* or *too modest.* You will never disobey Him by covering up *too much.*

If you find yourself choosing clothing from your closet asking, "I wonder if I can get away with this?," you are asking the wrong question. A better place to start is, "How can I honor Jesus most and protect my brothers with what I wear today?"

How low the cut is to the width of the straps. Two inches above the knee or fingertips long. Is it see-through or too tight? Is the message printed inappropriate or just the placement of it? Let's not even tackle bathing suits. I am sorry, ladies, in general, guys do not have to deal with this, and I am sure it can be maddening. Can I simplify things for you?

"If there is a part of your skin that you would be uncomfortable with me touching with my hand, I should not be able to see it with my eyes."

Man And *Wife* For Life

So God created man in his own image, in the image of God he created him; male and female he created them. (Gen. 1:27 ESV)

There are certainly homosexual acts, but not a *gay people*. We were all created in God's image. Scripture is clear that the Lord is against the *sin* of homosexuality (i.e., *Rom. 1*). It is not without choice, no different than any other immoral sin. It is true that a person can gravitate toward specific sin struggles in their life, but there is always the choice of obedience to God. He provides a way of escape from any temptation for the believer in whom the Holy Spirit dwells (*1 Cor. 10:13*).

It is just as evident in scripture God's design and plan for marriage (*Gen. 2*)—one man and one woman in a *committed* marriage covenant relationship for the rest of their lives. He recognized it was not good for man to be alone. In regard specifically to any burning sexual appetite, His solution is marriage (*1 Cor. 7*).

Many churches and pastors today are compromising biblical truth in the areas of both homosexuality as well as divorce. Current culture cannot keep us from agreeing with God on what He calls *sin*. I have heard it said, it would be *cruel* not to tell you the truth. God's people are supposed to be holy (i.e., *1 Pet. 1:16*), sanctified, and set apart. Yet the divorce rate in the church is mirroring that of the world.

I know there are many who would support there being biblical grounds for divorce (i.e., *Matt. 19*). Over my years as a pastor, I often needed to give grace to those I ministered to in broken marriages in the church. There are situations where help is immediately needed and real action has to take place to keep a family safe. But I stand against divorce, because God does. When I read passages like the end of *Ephesians 5* paralleling the husband-wife relationship to that of Christ and His bride, the church, I fail to believe there is any option of an *out* for me. When I read of the beautiful picture that is *Hosea*, imaging Christ's love, forgiveness, and forever faithfulness to me, there is nothing my wife could do that would alter the commitment I made to her on our wedding day before God and men. I will NEVER DIVORCE Erin.

> *And Pharisees came up to him and tested him by asking, "Is it lawful to divorce one's wife for any cause?" He answered, "Have you not read that he who created them from the beginning made them male and female, and said, 'Therefore a man shall leave his father and his mother and hold fast to his wife, and the two shall become one flesh'? So they are no longer two but one flesh. What therefore God has joined together, let not man separate." (Matt. 19:3–6 ESV)*

My Side Of Our Story

My wife is a godsend, a specific answer to a specific prayer. Thank you, Jesus.

During my time serving the Lord in Western Pennsylvania, I was committed to my singleness, especially during that season in life. I did not want a romantic relationship to "muddy the waters" of what God was doing in my heart. I had gotten it wrong so painfully in the past. I needed to focus on my relationship with the Lord apart from any distractions. Though I had options and certainly opportunities to date, I chose to just pray.

I wanted to be married, but I longed for Jesus more. I remember having the same conversation with the Lord night after night. "God, you know how badly I want to be married and my desire to honor you and remain pure. It cannot be me. It has to be you. I will wait on you, Lord. If your plan for me is marriage, I need it to be crystal clear that it is you. There can be no confusion. BRING HER TO MY DOOR."

My intensity in not failing in this area of my life again brought me to this recurring conversation that I don't think I truly understood what I was praying for. I lived in a building that required someone to buzz you in to enter. As I looked to the stars often through tear-filled eyes, heavyhearted, from my third-floor apartment balcony, I never thought to ask, "Okay, how are you going to bring her to my door?"

So I served, and I prayed. And I studied, and I grew. And I waited on Him. That was the most difficult, long, *sweet* time. I just fell more and more in love with Jesus.

One particular evening, I was excited to have some real down time. My place smelled of buttered popcorn, as I was setting up my stereo sound system to watch the newest Star Wars movie. I was determined to *feel* every laser come from those speakers. I was under the impression the apartment below me was vacant. It was a real spiritual bachelor moment. All I can say is, be ready, because at any time, God can show up.

A few minutes into my amazing media experience, there was a *POUNDING* on my door. I immediately grabbed the remote to mute the sound. I peeked out the little hole in the door to see a young brunette lady (not my wife) who was obviously upset. She knew I was there, and I totally chickened out and did not answer the door. I watched her leave annoyed. Moments later, like a weasel, I put my ear to the floor only to hear her call the front office and file a complaint against me.

I was going to run into her at some point. She lived in the apartment below me. Somehow, I had to get the upper hand. So I did what any "normal guy" would do. I threw on my shoes and my jacket, drove to the nearest grocery store, and twenty minutes later, knocked on her door with a dozen roses.

Knock, knock. "Who is it?"

"*It's your neighbor.*"

"Which one?"

"*The one you hate!*"

"I'm afraid to open the door."

"*Please, don't be.*"

As she slowly opened the door, my intent was truly to make amends for my mistake of avoiding the earlier conflict.

"*Hi. My name is Josh. I am pretty sure I upset you a while ago with the volume of my stereo. I went out and got these flowers for you, and I wanted to tell you how sorry I am. And I hope you will forgive me. If you have any other issues at all in the future, you don't even need to come up. I left my number in the flowers. Have a great night.*"

"Thanks."

I have to admit, as I walked back upstairs, I was feeling pretty good about myself. She was kind of pretty when she wasn't mad.

How could you be upset with anyone who just bought you a dozen roses? If nothing else, I had made a friend.

So, of course, like a weasel, I put my ear to the floor. I heard her call a girlfriend in excitement about a young guy upstairs that gave her flowers. I never did finish my movie or my popcorn. I went to bed, trusting God's sovereignty in it all.

About a week later, I was in the apartment complex workout facility, finishing up an exercise routine. My new neighbor walked in with a friend of hers just as I was ready to leave. I found out later they were both teachers. We smiled and waved, and as I was heading out the door, I paused suddenly to ask her a question. "Hey! Do you have any plans for Friday?"

She said, "No."

Then I replied with an even bigger smile than before, "Do you want some?" I realize now that I am older, I was not that smooth.

She smiled back and said, "Sure."

I invited her to call me when she was finished so we could discuss the details.

We had planned to do something very simple to get to know each other, coffee at a nearby Panera. I was terrified. I didn't know if this was of the Lord or just me, but I was so scared of screwing it up. I didn't even offer to drive her myself. She lived in the apartment below me, and I asked her to meet me there. What a gentleman.

As I drove, I talked with God. If she was a Christian, I wanted to know right away. And if she was not, I wanted her to know immediately what I was all about. I prayed the Holy Spirit would go before me and guide our conversation.

Within just a few minutes, I was boldly sharing the Gospel. She seemed disinterested in my faith as she stopped me mid-sentence and said, "Please, don't take this the wrong way. But you have to meet my friend." It had only been minutes, and she was already trying to pawn me off to someone else. Great first impression, Josh. Right?

Actually, I think it might have been. She began to "sales pitch" her good high school friend, Erin, with her blonde hair and blue eyes. She really worked hard at convincing me of her beauty. I was not leaning in on the conversation with full attention until she said, "She is just like you." Okay, that made me curious to hear more. Erin spent their high school years sharing her faith with her as well. I gathered she tried to point her to Jesus often. As we talked, it was kind of a big deal to hear someone who did not want anything to do with Christ and possibly did not even believe in sin, say these words, "It would be a *sin* for you two not to meet."

I surrendered the moment to the Lord, as she asked if it would be okay to pass my contact information on to her high school friend. I said, "That would be okay." As we got up to leave our short time together, she turned to say, "Oh, I just want to let you know, Erin took a teaching position in Southern Ohio, about five hours away."

Can I tell you something? If you are looking for purity in a dating relationship, I strongly suggest dating someone who lives five hours away from you. It is a foolproof plan. It is not what I would have naturally wanted, but I had learned to want what God wants. And He knew exactly what He was doing.

Do you remember AOL Instant Messenger? That was the online chat platform, nearly eighteen years ago, on which I had my first conversation with the woman I so deeply love today. I did not know when Erin "broke the ice" and said hello for the first time, how it would forever change my life. Afterward, I didn't run into my neighbor that often at all, but she was a part of our wedding party. She was Erin's good friend. God used her to bring us together. And I knew she would hear the Gospel at least one more time at our ceremony.

Erin and I lived far from each other, though ironically we both resided in each other's home state. We were forced to talk. It was all we had, and it never got old. We would share our love for music, sports, family, and most of all, Jesus. I could not get enough of her God stories. They stirred my faith. My interest level only increased in the pure safety of our distance. IMs led to the sharing of photos and mail. Soon, we would only be satisfied with the sound of the other's voice over the phone. FREE NIGHTS AND WEEKENDS. The old folks reading this will understand and remember that cell phone plan. We were falling for each other, with the hopes of what God might do with our future.

We planned to meet face-to-face for the first time as she would visit her family (one of the next towns over) for the holidays just a few months out. My prayer had not changed. "Bring her to my door." Neither of us knew anything for sure yet, and we were seeking the Lord.

I had just gotten home on a Sunday afternoon after singing and preaching at a small church in Western Pennsylvania. It was a blessed service. I kicked off my shoes and was removing my tie as the phone rang. It was Erin. Still to this day, she is an avid Steelers fan. My team has always been the Browns. We are a "house divided." After I picked up the telephone and we said hello, this is how the rest of the conversation went,

"How was service this morning?"

"*It went really well, thank you.*"

"You're welcome. Do you have the game on?"

"*Oh, that's right! I totally forgot they were playing each other today. Let me turn it on now.*"

"Okay. Well, do you mind if I come up and watch it with you?"

"*Oh, sure. Wait! What?*"

"Look out your window."

As I pulled the blinds and saw her beauty as she waved from the parking lot three stories down, *I FREAKED OUT.* I paused for a moment to "size her up" and determine if I could take her in a fight, in case she was an axe murderer. Ha! In nervous excitement, I requested five minutes to clean my place up. I was a single guy, not prepared for company. In my frantic state, I think I remember putting dirty dishes in the fridge and maybe even dirty laundry in the oven. It all happened so suddenly, and she was so sweet to surprise me. I buzzed her into the building. Moments later, there was a knock at the door. Even now as I write and attempt to deliver memory to page, it is difficult to hold the tears back. Our God is so good.

The Lord brought her to my door. I was in awe of how beautiful she was to me. She was attractive, but it was *who* she was and her love for Jesus that took my breath away. I felt like I was just meeting someone I had already known really well for quite some time. As we both smiled from ear to ear with the excitement of the moment, I knew there was only one thing to say. "I need you to trust me. We have to get out of here and go somewhere public (*2 Tim. 2:22*)." She giggled a bit and with complete understanding, agreed.

We had dinner overlooking the runway of a nearby small airport. It was very romantic. One of the most fun times I have ever had during a meal. I knew without a shadow of a doubt, this was worth pursuing. We prayed together and asked the Lord for guidance in our newfound relationship. It was difficult to be so far away. We would only visit a weekend every couple of months. We never really spent any significant amount of time together, until we were married.

I was committed to not asking Erin's hand in marriage until we had dated at least a year. There was much-needed wisdom in not rushing. Erin is in her eighteenth year of teaching music at the high school and collegiate level. Early in her career, I surprised her in a tux with her own bouquet of roses, as she thought I was in another state. Her parents were in Pennsylvania eagerly waiting for us to call, while the school administration was secretly helping me pull off *"project proposal."* I serenaded her on stage at the end of her choir concert, in front of all of her students and their parents. On bended knee, I asked her to marry me. With shaking excitement, she said yes.

We were married nearly a year later. I decided it was in my best interest to actually live with my new wife, so I headed back to Ohio. Over another fifteen years married with four children, two homes and nine vehicles, with nearly a combined twenty years of vocational ministry experience, as well as now one book, the rest as they say is history. I am so undeserving of God's great grace, but I am so incredibly thankful for it.

Love Letters

"If you have struggled in a past dating relationship, failed to remain pure in your walk with Christ, or maybe given your eyes, thoughts, and heart away to pornography, you may feel *BROKEN*, but you are not *UNUSABLE*. Please, do not fall into the trap of believing that if you have stepped outside of God's plan and design for marriage, you might as well stay there. Repent of your sin and commit to the Lord to do things His way moving forward. Commit now to your future spouse your purity and your faithfulness, lifting them up in prayer each day from now on."

On the last teaching session of a series like this, I will usually incorporate some tangible, visual exercise that will allow the students to physically get up and move and take action as they commit new choices, fresh to the Lord. Once, I had a huge basin of water, color-dyed red. The students wrote with red ink on small pieces of paper sin struggles they desired to surrender to Christ. As a part of the worship service, they were given the opportunity to respond by taking what they had written, attaching a weighted paper clip, and dropping them into the water. As "Christ's blood covered their mistakes," the written sins would vanish (*Heb. 9:22*) in the red water as the paper would sink to the bottom of the basin.

Another time, a group I had was outside near a pond. I had gathered a large pile of small stones earlier. This time, they were given the opportunity to write on the stones. We tied this exercise in with the passage of scripture telling of the woman caught in the act of adultery and Jesus' response to the crowd who were all equally sinners. He was the only one there who could forgive sins. As they dispersed, leaving their stones behind on the ground, Jesus told the woman to "sin no more" (*John 8:11*). This was another "altar" opportunity for these students to make life-changing decisions before God, as they "cast their sins" deep into the pond, only to walk pure in Christ in the days ahead.

The use of a consuming fire is another great idea. You could do anything you want really. Whether it is a group of students or adults, an individual who is single or married, or you are a parent working with your own child. There is just something about a physical action creating a picture along with a heart decision that solidifies a commitment moment.

After this is when I ask every student in the group to participate in one final activity, I believe to be the most important. I will provide an ambiance with quiet music, as well as writing materials, with nice card stock and manila envelopes. This is all part of the worship service as well. I will ask them to write a letter to their future spouse, vowing their purity from this day forward. I'll usually tease the guys a bit to make sure they use their neatest handwriting, so their future wives can read it. After the letter is completed and sealed in the envelope, the gentlemen are to give it to their fathers and the ladies to their mothers. This gets the crucial accountability conversations going with the parents. Mom and Dad are then to keep the letter safe until their child's wedding day, when they hand deliver it to their new son-/daughter-in-law. If taken seriously, this can be life changing.

Parents, consider doing this (or something like this) with your kids. Adults, single or married, you can do this yourselves. Commit your purity from this day forward to the Lord. Commit your purity from this day forward to your future or current spouse. No matter your past or even your current situation in this area of your Christian life, God can *use* your *brokenness* for His glory, if you will surrender it to Him.

Example Student Letter

Hi Honey,

We may not have even met yet, but I want you to know that I am praying for you every day. I cannot wait to see what God is going to do when He brings us together. I have recently been challenged to write to you on this day, 10/18/21, to vow before God my purity to you alone, today and every day after. My heart is yours. My thoughts belong to you. I will have eyes only for you, Sweetheart. I promise you this, to honor our Lord and to strengthen our marriage, to the glory of God. I am waiting for you, and I am so excited to marry you.

Love you always,
Joshua A. Hales

SCENE 3

This Is The Pits

If God allowed you to lose everything, how would you respond? Your ministry. Your career and financial stability. Your position and influence. Your home and all your belongings. Your family and friends. Your health and the ability to care for even just yourself. If you were left with nothing but your salvation (your eternal security found in the shed blood of Jesus), would He be enough?

We all experience the ups and downs of life. The mountain peaks of blessing and the valleys of struggle. Not many of us will have to face a life journey so broken that it *forces* our heart to answer the question of whether or not we are fully satisfied in Christ.

What do you do when tragedy shakes your faith, when death knocks at your home's door, when you have been betrayed by those you call family, or when you are innocent but trapped in a series of lies and gossip that destroys your reputation? How do you recover when you are blindsided, your "teeth get kicked in" and no one has your back? When you have been faithful to the Lord, but you are left with nothing but questions?

These few vague examples barely touch on the brokenness of our world caused by sin. I want to encourage you, one day God will right all wrongs. He knows the truth. He is the Truth (*John 14:6*). There are times I am left without answers to the big questions I have for God. Though I do not *know* the answers, I have learned to rest in the truth that I know the one who knows. None of "this stuff" matters in light of eternity. There will come a day I will be face-to-face with my Savior, forever in the presence of the Lord. Today, I choose to find my FULL satisfaction in Jesus Christ and in Him alone.

Never More Broken

We were newlyweds, "serving our britches off" in our first church, ascending one of those mountain peaks of blessing. We did not see the *pit* coming afar off, but we fell into it nonetheless. God was (and is) still faithful.

Erin and I both were a part of the church choir and praise team and would help lead worship. We were actively involved in our young married's group that I taught from time to time. We found our passion in volunteering with the students, as I led the junior high ministry. Young people and their families were coming to the saving knowledge of Jesus Christ, and we were so humbled the Lord would use us in any way to advance His Kingdom. To God be the Glory.

It was not long until I was called to my first pastoral position in local church ministry. I was hired on staff at the church where we were already serving. We were honored. God was moving. Every day was hands-on education for me—children and students; adult groups and seniors; sports evangelism and outreach; worship and teaching; missions and preaching; visitation, funerals, and weddings; PASTORING. Each day came with some degree of uncertainty as well as excitement amid the on-the-job training. We were where God wanted us to be, doing what He put us on this Earth to do. Life was good.

Several years later, we were expecting even greater things from the Lord, because we were expecting our firstborn son, Connor. He was just six months old when we stepped away from that ministry, too young to remember our family's first church. The events that followed kept us out of vocational ministry for a lengthy season that felt like an eternity.

The day Connor came into this world was the first day I was severely sick. At first, it was joked that I could not *handle* childbirth, but then I only got worse. It was summer, not flu season, so we weren't sure what the cause was. Out of necessity, I left my newborn and my healing wife at the hospital to visit our family physician. I was given a prescription for anti-nausea medication, but it didn't really help. We still had no answers as to what was going on with my body. One of the most joyous occasions of my life was spent ill, empty, and weak. I could not hold anything down. I was suffering from malnutrition and dehydration. As my neck muscles strained from all the vomiting, I had no voice due to the aggressive acid.

We took our son home, and I wasn't getting any better. Days became weeks. Weeks became months. I saw a digestive specialist. He did all he could, running every test in textbook order. Ultrasounds. Scans. They would look at the gut, finding no answers. They'd eventually hunt for tumors in my brain that did not exist. I'd be put to sleep, with cameras in my body. They would ask me to drink or eat large amounts of radioactive food, and it would be required that I'd hold it down long enough for them to receive necessary imaging. That was torture. No one could figure it out. I would seek help from multiple doctors, only to be told that that was unwise by the same doctors without answers.

Every test ran produced the same result. There was "nothing wrong" with me. I was "perfectly healthy." It was even suggested that perhaps it was all in my head, and the proper course of action could be to see a therapist. I'm a pastor, and I am an advocate for counseling. But there was nothing I was going to *talk* about that would keep what was happening from happening. It was not in my head. It was in my belly, and it was killing me.

Soon I would spend every day all day throwing up. I'd lose food most often. Sometimes I would just dry heave. In case you didn't know, that's not normal. It is not good for you to walk around with the pressure and pain equal to that of lying belly down with your full-body weight on top of a tennis ball. That's how I felt every moment of every day. And vomiting became as natural as breathing for me after a while. It was my new normal. I could not do anything to relieve that pressure, but the pain would fractionally subside with each episode of getting sick. Smells would trigger an episode. Dinner. A diaper. Even just talking would trigger my gag reflex and fire off an always loaded cannon. And every time it happened, I would feel more defeated. In complete transparency, I was so broken, I didn't even think about how defeated Erin must have felt.

Before we stepped down from my position at the church, I would have to teach the students seated, with a wastebasket by my side. It was so uncomfortable for me (and for them) when I would need to use it in the middle of a lesson. We would be heading to a service project or youth event, and I would frequently pull the church van over to get sick on the side of the road. My declining health made it impossible to do what I loved and what I *knew* God had called me to. I didn't understand. Why was He allowing this to happen?

In total, I had seen seven doctors for my digestive problems, not including multiple emergency room visits—two family practice physicians and five digestive specialists. Two of those were from the same local practice, though four of the five would repeat all the same tests, only to produce the same inconclusive results. I remember thinking I would be okay to find out I had cancer, because at least I would know an answer and a possible course of treatment. They weren't finding anything wrong with me. One was a surgeon, and the final doctor was not local, a specialist practicing at the Cleveland Clinic.

The first specialist I had seen put me on an acid reflux medication. This was much-needed, and I still take that prescription today. But stomach acid is a part of the digestion process. My acid is "turned off" because it was causing me more problems than it was helping break down food. I was *misdiagnosed* by another doctor and put on a risky medication that *can* cause Parkinson's. I had to sign paperwork saying I would not sue the practice if that were to happen to me because of the meds. It was his belief that my stomach muscles had become paralyzed and that the *side effects* of this medicine would improve things.

Shortly after, the Cleveland Clinic doctor determined my misdiagnosis and immediately took me off that prescription. I do not believe any damage was done in the way of Parkinson's. Praise God! At some point, I was put on a second anti-nausea medication. Additionally, I was prescribed a low dose of an antidepressant, again for the benefits of the side effects that particular medication could *possibly* produce. I didn't take that very long. Like everything else, it didn't help.

The surgeon, per my request, ran a more unique scan of the functionality of my gallbladder, rather than just imaging of what it looked like. It was not working properly. Given the test results and that they were the only "answer" found that could even pertain to my illness, it was time to have my gallbladder removed. It's not "needed," but it does help break down specific types of foods, oils and greases. I was scheduled for laparoscopic surgery to once again eliminate another piece of my digestive system that God originally had given me. There were complications during surgery, and I was cut open instead, left with a seven-/eight-inch scar across my torso. *I was in a knife fight, and I lost.* I still have nerve damage causing a fist-sized section of my flesh to have no feeling at all. Due to the complications and change in procedures, my recovery in the hospital took a week, rather than just a couple days as planned. I missed my wife and my son.

As I continued to heal at home over some time, I was convinced we had discovered the problem and that I was fixed. I *hoped* we had removed what was broken inside me. I was doing much better, and God had blessed us with our second son, Nolan. When Connor was very young and Nolan was still a baby, my illness came back more aggressive than ever. It was like a recurring nightmare. Starting over again, with the same doctors without answers, we continued to try to figure out what was wrong with me. That was the hardest part for me, not knowing. I knew God knew, but I didn't. It wasn't fair.

But He doesn't promise life will be fair, does He? I didn't understand what God was doing. I knew He had rescued me many years before, only to put me on His path leading to the Gospel ministry. What was I going to do for the Lord in bed sick all the time? I wasn't mad at God. I knew what that felt like already. This was not that. This was an overwhelming sense of questions without answers. I took them to the Lord every day. He chose not to answer in my timing but rather taught me many hard life lessons I did not realize I needed to learn. God was (and is) still faithful.

Lessons Learned

My Heavenly Father loves me more than I will ever understand.

It was not until I became a father myself that I could even skim the surface of understanding God's love for me.

One morning, I was very ill and pouty and just not pleasant to be around. I was not Kingdom-focused at all. I was Josh-focused. It was easy to do when I was so sick and even easier to go a few days without spending time with the Lord or studying His Word. I was pretty self-absorbed that morning, and my heart was in a dark place. Trusting Him was not on my radar, and I just did not want any responsibilities.

Connor was young and had previously gotten a shot at the doctor's on his thigh. I had to get him ready for the day. As we were changing his clothes, I noticed his Band-Aid that had been there for a while. The adhesive had gathered dirt. His leg needed cleaning, and the bandage needed to be removed and discarded. He was not interested in that.

As I took on the task of caring for my son the way I knew he needed, his response was as if he was having his arms ripped off. We wrestled a bit as he screamed through his tears. His fear of the unknown removed all sane thought. I was the enemy, and he would not let me cause him pain. I knew what he needed, and I was loving him through the difficult challenge. My frustration had maxed out as I removed the Band-Aid. He slowly calmed down, gaining control of his emotions again, as we talked through what had just happened.

"Son, do you not trust me? Don't you know how much I love you? I would never hurt you. I am trying to help you. There are reasons this had to happen, and you need to trust that I know what it is you need. I am for you. I am not against you." As we hugged it out, Connor wiped his last couple of tears on the shoulder of my T-shirt. I held him just a little bit tighter as he looked up and pointed to the top shelf of the bookcase. "Can we read my Bible, please?"

"All right, Lord. Message received loud and clear."

Thank you therapy.

I still needed to learn and develop an attitude of gratitude.

I was sitting patiently in the Cleveland Clinic waiting room. I stayed at my parents' home for a couple of days to make my appointment. I felt like garbage. I sat there waiting, wondering what I had already wondered for so long. Would we ever figure this out? Was I ever going to get better? I closed my eyes to pray a half-hearted prayer with little faith behind it.

When I opened my eyes again, across the aisle from me sat a man with gray-colored skin, missing an arm. Almost immediately, just a couple of seats down, sat another man missing the opposite arm. Within seconds, a nurse helped a third man in a wheelchair find his place at the end of the row of seats. He had no legs. I began to survey the entire waiting room of people, quickly realizing that my situation could have been so much worse.

The hours in the car driving back home flew by, as I spent them thanking God for all the blessings I could think of in my life. It was not enough time. Upon my return home, I continued to journal many lists for several days, all that I was thankful to God for. It refocused my heart and helped me tremendously during the rest of my illness.

Social media ministry.

I spent a lot of time on social media providing updates and giving reports on my health. I was home sick so often. I needed to connect with people somehow. To know that many were praying for me and our family was powerful. The impact was immeasurable, but I assumed it only went one direction.

I would give weekly, sometimes daily news on test results and doctor's visits. I'd pull back the curtain quite a bit, sharing how often and severely sick I would get. To tell of my drastic weight loss was concerning to say the least. But no matter how difficult any given day was or how negative a report I might have shared, I always gave God glory and ended each post with the words, "God is good!" I think I almost had to force myself to do it so that I would keep believing the truth of those words.

Later, I would come to find out how so many were not only encouraged but were able to keep going on in their own personal health struggles. Their faith was rejuvenated by mine. I had no idea. Some told me that they didn't think they could handle going through what I had gone through. After witnessing my journey, they grew confident that they then knew how to handle something similar if it ever happened to them. God used my experience to help others. I pray He does the same on an even grander scale through this book.

Not many things are more important than family.

If nothing else good came from my illness, I was blessed God reminded me of my need for complete dependency on Him. In my lifetime, when God seemed furthest away, those were the times I drew closest to the Lord. I don't know how to explain how the most difficult times can feel the most blessed. I want so badly the intimacy and the closeness I experience with God just as much during the mountain peaks of life as in those valley lows.

The intimacy and closeness I experienced with family during my illness was nearly as important. I loved my wife and our children more intensely than ever. God used that difficult chapter in our lives to draw us closer to Him and to each other. Even the relationships with our extended families grew deeper. It helped us support one another in unity as the tides became more rapid. I was getting sicker than I had ever been, and our entire extended family's faith was about to be refined.

"No More, Please!"

I lost eighty pounds in four months' time without trying. I was literally starving to death.

I suppose I was grateful to be a heavier set guy. Even an average-sized adult male would not have easily recovered from such drastic weight loss. I was smaller than in my best condition as a wrestler in high school. I was so sick, and I felt worthless. I knew we were running out of time.

Erin was such a huge support for me—my biggest cheerleader. I don't think I could have gotten through it without her. But as her husband, I needed to have the most difficult discussion I would ever have with her. "Honey, we might still figure this out. It may be a simple 'push of a button.' But if we don't figure out which 'button to push' in time, you have to be ready. I am only getting worse. If I'm on track to lose another eighty pounds in the next four months, I won't make it. I will die."

I broke her. All the same defeat and anxiety I had felt each day for so long, she held onto. It unraveled in that moment. She sobbed. I cried too as I excused myself to get sick again. We prayed together. Later that evening, I visited and talked with a pastor friend. Even later in the evening, I talked with God by myself. As my family slept, I pleaded with the Lord. I could not handle anything else. I never felt so alone.

Days later, Erin was taking the trash out and slipped on our icy deck. I should have salted it. I was weak and not accomplishing much around the house. My wife dislocated her shoulder. She could no longer pick up our baby until she healed. It was up to me now to help her no matter how sick I was at any given moment whenever she and Nolan needed me. I would change diapers without hope of not getting sick, oftentimes barely able to stand.

Then I got the call. It was Dad. There were complications during a medical procedure Mom had undergone, and she suffered a severe stroke. They were keeping her alive, as she unconsciously continued to have seizures. The family needed me in Cleveland. I had to get there right away if I wanted the chance to say goodbye to my mother. I could not believe this was all happening.

Erin's mom was so gracious to take time off work and travel from Pennsylvania without any real notice. Erin needed help. I got in the car just as quickly and drove all the way to Cleveland, with tear-filled eyes and a wastebasket in my lap. It was probably not safe for me to drive under such conditions. I had thrown up many times while crying the entire four-hour-long trip. In complete brokenness and selfishness, I cried out to God in the car, "No more, please! I don't understand. Why are you letting this happen? If you are done with me, just take me home." I had a wife and two children at the time that needed a healthy daddy to come back to them. I regretted those words ever left my mouth as soon as I heard myself say them.

When I arrived at the hospital, I cleaned my face, took both my anti-nausea meds, and prepared to wear my "pastor's hat" and minister to my family as best I could. Dad was exhausted. I could not let any of them know how exhausted I was as well. I had to be strong for them. I saw my mom for the first time in the ICU, with one side of her face *not right* and wires and tubes sticking out from every part of her body. I held her "lifeless" hand as I spoke with her, hopeful that somehow she could hear me and feel my presence. Shortly after, I excused myself to the bathroom, where I privately lost control of my emotions and again got aggressively sick.

The Favorite Son

By now, you've probably realized how much I like a good story. We all do. We wonder what is to come of the *once upon a time*, and we celebrate the *happily ever after*. We love to see *good* overcome *evil*, and who can't appreciate a victorious *underdog* tale? Even Jesus preached in parables, telling earthly stories with Heavenly meaning. When I was sick, I would spend much of my time with the Lord in prayer, and I would study and restudy one of the Bible's greatest stories—the real-life account of Joseph.

He was the eleventh son in a broken home situation, same father, but multiple mothers. Joseph was the son of Jacob (Israel), the grandson of Isaac, and the great grandson of Abraham (the patriarch of the Jewish nation). Remember, what we do as parents directly affects our kids. God used these men despite their legacy passed down of polygamy and deception, unfaithful to the Lord's plan and timing. I have learned that evil compiled with evil usually produces more evil. Joseph was the product of God's perfect plan in motion behind the scenes.

God used young people in the Old Testament, and He still uses them today. In *Genesis 37*, with his seventeen-year-old heart full of expectation of what the Lord might do in and through him, Joseph approached great evil—the first unforeseen *pit* of many to come. He followed his dreams and was faithful to the Lord, no matter what. God had his hands on this young man and took some time to prepare him in the most difficult ways for the events to happen many years later.

Jacob loved Joseph more than his brothers (*v. 3*). There was no greater evidence of his favoritism than that of gifting Joseph his multicolored robe. We don't know much about the coat, but we do know it was meant to signify that he was special from all the others. Not good parenting. His brothers hated him so much that they couldn't even talk to the guy (*v. 4*). I have to believe Joseph was not naive, and he realized how each family member felt about him. No one was tiptoeing around their feelings, good or bad. He must have been aware of the animosity of his siblings.

Joseph was a dreamer. God had given him dreams and the ability to interpret dreams. He probably would have been better served not to be so open with the family about what the Lord had shown him. They would all bow down to him some day. I can only imagine how well that conversation went over. Jacob rebuked him, but his brothers only grew in hatred and jealousy. (*vs. 5–11*)

Soon after, Joseph found himself on a journey to Shechem. Jacob charged Joseph to bring him a report on his brothers and their care of the family's flock, similar to that in *verse 2*. He stopped to "ask for directions," learning his brothers had gone to Dothan, over sixty miles from home. He found them there, without the protection of his father, plotting against him. (*vs. 12–17*)

> *They saw him from afar, and before he came near to them they conspired against him to kill him. They said to one another, "Here comes this dreamer. Come now, let us kill him and throw him into one of the pits. Then we will say that a fierce animal has devoured him, and we will see what will become of his dreams." But when Reuben heard it, he rescued him out of their hands, saying, "Let us not take his life." And Reuben said to them, "Shed no blood; throw him into this pit here in the wilderness, but do not lay a hand on him"—that he might rescue him out of their hand to restore him to his father. (Gen. 37:18–22 ESV)*

Joseph's brothers were committed to his premeditated murder. They hated him. They would ensure his dreams would never come true. I can't even imagine one of my sons ever hating their brother so much that they would be willing to kill him. That would devastate me. We see the same thing earlier in *Genesis 4* when Cain killed Abel. I guarantee Adam and Eve's immediate response was not to pick up a pen and start writing history's first parenting book. What must they have felt as parents, especially being responsible for sin entering into the world?

Reuben seemed to have some reasoning, some sense about him. At least his love for his father was greater than his hate for his brother. He fully intended to rescue Joseph and bring him safely back to his dad. He convinced the other brothers not to harm Joseph but simply trap him in a pit. When Reuben temporarily left the scene apparently, Judah led the others in a plan to profit off of Joseph.

> *So when Joseph came to his brothers, they stripped him of his robe, the robe of many colors that he wore. And they took him and threw him into a pit. The pit was empty; there was no water in it.*
>
> *Then they sat down to eat. And looking up they saw a caravan of Ishmaelites coming from Gilead, with their camels bearing gum, balm, and myrrh, on their way to carry it down to Egypt. Then Judah said to his brothers, "What profit is it if we kill our brother and conceal his blood? Come, let us sell him to the Ishmaelites, and let not our hand be upon him, for he is our brother, our own flesh." And his brothers listened to him. Then Midianite traders passed by. And they drew Joseph up and lifted him out of the pit, and sold him to the Ishmaelites for twenty shekels of silver. They took Joseph to Egypt.*
> *(Gen. 37:23–28 ESV)*

How intense their hatred for Joseph must have been, to throw him in a pit he could not escape, with no water to drink, and they sat down together for a meal. After a brief bidding war between the Ishmaelites and the Midianites, they sold young Joseph into slavery. Joseph *pleaded* with his brothers (*Gen. 42:21*), but they were *done* with him. As they pocketed the silver, Joseph had a long and difficult journey ahead. I am certain he had a number of unanswered questions for the Lord. But even as a slave in Egypt, God was faithful in the life of Joseph.

The church must be *known* for its character of grace, mercy, forgiveness, unity, and love. The world will know we are His disciples by our love for one another (*John 13:35*). As a follower of Christ, I cannot be known for *hate*. The Bible teaches that hate is murder of the heart (*1 John 3:15*). I hope I am never guilty of "throwing someone into the pit." I pray God always helps me demonstrate His attributes. The world needs nothing greater than the love of Jesus.

Joseph was purchased from the Ishmaelites by Potiphar, the captain of the guard, an officer of Pharaoh (*Gen 39:1*). It was clear that *God was with Joseph*, and Potiphar recognized it immediately (*v. 3*). I am sure Joseph missed his father and his little brother, Benjamin, but this ended up being a "best-case scenario" for the slave, given the circumstances. Though he probably wondered often how God would use his situation to see his gifted dreams come to fruition, Joseph was raised to a prestigious position over Potiphar's house (*v. 4*). Because of Joseph, God blessed everything Potiphar had. Joseph was in charge of it all (*v. 5*), receiving great experience for future leadership opportunities. The only thing Potiphar needed to worry about was feeding himself (*v. 6*). Wow!

> *And after a time his master's wife cast her eyes on Joseph and said, "Lie with me." But he refused and said to his master's wife, "Behold, because of me my master has no concern about anything in the house, and he has put everything that he has in my charge. He is not greater in this house than I am, nor has he kept back anything from me except you, because you are his wife. How then can I do this great wickedness and sin against God?" And as she*

spoke to Joseph day after day, he would not listen to her, to lie beside her or to be with her.

But one day, when he went into the house to do his work and none of the men of the house was there in the house, she caught him by his garment, saying, "Lie with me." But he left his garment in her hand and fled and got out of the house. And as soon as she saw that he had left his garment in her hand and had fled out of the house, she called to the men of her household and said to them, "See, he has brought among us a Hebrew to laugh at us. He came in to me to lie with me, and I cried out with a loud voice. And as soon as he heard that I lifted up my voice and cried out, he left his garment beside me and fled and got out of the house." Then she laid up his garment by her until his master came home, and she told him the same story, saying, "The Hebrew servant, whom you have brought among us, came in to me to laugh at me. But as soon as I lifted up my voice and cried, he left his garment beside me and fled out of the house." (Gen. 39:7–18 ESV)

Even as a slave without answers to so many questions, Joseph was faithful to the Lord. It was Potiphar's wife enticing him, but his greatest concern was to not sin against *God*. This lady wouldn't let up. She was immoral and a liar. It was her sin that caused even greater problems for Joseph. He was committed to purity and as Scripture teaches, ran from immorality. He was left cloakless again, about to be thrown into another *pit*.

Potiphar's wife was furious with Joseph's repeated rejection. She devised her own "on-the-spot" agenda. She "dragged Joseph's name in the mud," claiming attempted rape before he fled in fear because of her screams for help. His reputation was ruined by these false accusations. He was innocent but seen as a criminal to be captured and prosecuted. I just want to reach into the Scriptures and give Joseph a hug. He deserved a break.

The Bible does not say this, but I believe Potiphar *knew* his wife and doubted her story from the beginning. He also knew Joseph. Potiphar was a powerful leader, and the laws of that day and land were clear. Joseph should have been killed, but Potiphar threw him into prison instead (*vs. 20*). Joseph was still alive—*broken* but still *usable*. It may not have seemed like it at that moment, but God was faithful in the life of Joseph.

We are all susceptible to any type of sin. My heart is saddened when I hear of a pastor or church leader who falls to immorality. When true repentance takes place, it is our responsibility as the body of Christ to forgive and come alongside them (and their families) to help walk them through whatever the restoration process may look like. It breaks my heart even more when godly men are *TORN* from ministry leadership because of the false accusations of divisive people in the church. When God's hand is *clearly* on an individual, who for whatever reason has not met your personal expectations, please do not lie, gossip, and falsely destroy their reputation. Forget your agenda.

When God is in it, pay attention. When it is obvious the Lord is blessing the ministry of a pastor or church leader, don't get behind a man. Get behind God. When there is any issue with that leader, go to them one-on-one (*Matt. 18:15*). If need be, bring another trusted leader in the church along. *A good rule of thumb is to not talk about anyone negatively if they are not in the room.* Determine to have that conversation in a spirit of unity. I know that is not always easy, but it is godly.

The Lord had a plan for Joseph's life, no matter who brought their sin into the picture to try to mess it up. God was with him even in the prison (*vs. 21*). Joseph was once again raised to a position of management by the jail keeper, because it was obvious to him as well that God's hand was on Joseph (*vs. 22*)—another "best-case scenario" in horrific circumstances. He was in charge of all the prisoners. Everything Joseph did in the prison needed *no* supervision and was a complete success (*vs. 23*). He continued to grow in the Lord and in leadership.

Sometimes, God opens doors for opportunities, not because of what we know but perhaps *who* we know. Joseph was in charge of two prisoners (the king's chief cupbearer and chief baker), both probably accused of attempting to poison Pharaoh (*Gen. 40:1–4*). One was innocent and the other guilty. Both had dreams. Joseph was a dreamer. One morning, Joseph could tell they were troubled. He could see it in their faces (*vs. 6–7*). They shared with Joseph their dreams, and he interpreted them each, giving God the glory (*vs. 8–19*). Then Pharaoh restored the cupbearer to his previous position but hanged the baker, just as God had revealed to Joseph what would happen through the interpretation of the dreams.

Joseph's faithfulness to the Lord and the fact that God's favor never left him did not mean he was happy in the pit of prison. He was not staying at a Hilton. He trusted God's plan and timing, but he still wanted out. He did nothing to deserve the punishments for which he was paying.

> *"Only remember me, when it is well with you, and please do me the kindness to mention me to Pharaoh, and so get me out of this house. For I was indeed stolen out of the land of the Hebrews, and here also I have done nothing that they should put me into the pit." (Gen. 40:14–15 ESV)*

He asked the chief cupbearer to remember him when restored to his position in the palace. Joseph was hopeful the cupbearer's relationship with Pharaoh could influence his release from jail.

> *Yet the chief cupbearer did not remember Joseph, but forgot him. (Gen. 40:23 ESV)*

Two years went by before Joseph ever crossed the cupbearer's mind. It was not until Pharaoh himself was deeply troubled after having two similar dream experiences as the former prisoners (*Gen. 41:1–7*). But no one in Egypt was able to help him understand what they meant (*vs. 8*). Finally, the chief cupbearer remembered his imprisonment with Joseph and gave him the referral of his lifetime (*vs. 9–13*).

The Bible is silent on the two years Joseph was forgotten in prison. I wonder at times if those years were the most difficult in Joseph's story. With all he had already gone through in life, was that the hardest thing to be forgotten? Have you ever felt forgotten? I know I have. I want to speak truth into your life right now. God is with you. He always has been. He always will be (*Matt. 28:20b*). Though you may feel left, alone, mistreated, and forgotten, God has a purpose in it all. Trust Him, and wait on the Lord. Remembering His faithfulness in the past will give you the confidence that He will remain faithful now and forever.

If anyone can understand what God allowed Joseph to go through, it is Jesus. He was loved by His Father and hated by those around Him. Sold. Falsely accused. Did nothing wrong but punished for the sins of those He came to save. Joseph was the great grandson of Abraham, through whom God covenanted He would make a great nation. The Lord promised to bless his family. So Abraham had Isaac, and Isaac had Jacob. Joseph was one of Jacob's twelve sons, the leaders of the twelve tribes of Israel. God chose Joseph to save the nation of Israel during extreme famine. God chose the nation of Israel to bring about the Messiah, whom God chose to bring about His redemptive plan for the World. *I am saved today because of God's faithfulness in the life of Joseph.* Hallelujah!

To be continued…

God Was (And Is) Still Faithful

God is good! Not because of what He does or does not do but simply because of who He is.

I cannot find my full satisfaction in a ministry position or the influence that may come with it, not in financial stability or the belongings it affords me. I can't find it in the blessings of family or relationships. It is not found in personal health or in that of those I love most. My *FULL SATISFACTION* must be in Jesus Christ and in Him alone. If God allowed me to be left with nothing but my salvation, I would still have everything.

My wife's shoulder healed. Life was soon normal again for her and the kids. Her mom traveled back to Pennsylvania, and I came home after days with my family in the hospital. I fully expected to see them again soon for Mom's funeral. Through the power of thousands praying, I believe God gave us a miracle. Moment by moment, hour by hour, and day by day, hope grew within our family. Mom was getting better. Every report I received from a distance brought me to happy tears and a full heart of thankfulness.

The next time I saw her in the hospital, she had never looked more beautiful. It was a long therapy-filled first year for Mom. We were all so happy she was still with us. Not a single railing installation or self-home therapy routine was inconvenient for anyone. She couldn't drive herself to appointments, but that just allowed more time and conversation in the car to reflect on God's goodness. One of my greatest privileges in life was to witness my dad's tenderness in the hospital and care for his wife. Although my mother still *feels* it very real and in different ways each day, *you* would not know she had a stroke unless one of us told you. Thank you, Lord.

My local doctor who had misdiagnosed me came across a shared report from the Cleveland Clinic practice. The numbers were pre-borderline deficient concerning digestive enzymes of the pancreas, specific to a stool sample test that was run. It was nothing anyone would have normally paid any attention to, if they had even recognized it. This local digestive specialist wanted to try something. He said, "I am going to write you a prescription. If it helps, we know what is wrong. If it does not help, then you can stop taking it almost right away."

The script was not medicine. It was for supplemental digestive enzymes from the pancreas of a pig. Apparently, these enzymes are necessary to break down food. For unknown reasons, my pancreas stopped producing them. Many pig organs are similar to that of humans. I was diagnosed with chronic pancreatitis, not necessarily because of tests but because of treatment. When I took those pills for the very first time, I COULD EAT AGAIN. "Hello, pizza, my old friend." I had developed a new, deep, personal love for the *pig*. Who knew "bacon could actually save your life?" I will always have to take these pills every time I eat, but so what. Second only to complete healing is maintaining health through medicine. Just as miraculous.

I am in awe of God's beautiful design and creation of the human body itself, almost as much as its ability to compensate and recover from what can be lost from its original blueprint when injured or damaged from illness. Mom did not die. I am still alive. God is so good. But if He had taken her or allowed my wife to be a widow with two young sons and if my youngest boy and daughter were never to exist, He would still be just as good. If the many years to follow of our family's Gospel ministry never happened, He'd still be God. It's not about me. It's not about us. It is all about Him. *If I can trust Him for my eternity, I can trust Him for my today.*

SCENE 4

Endless Forgiveness

Early in my ministry, I directed a community outreach program, a men's basketball league of over one hundred and twenty recreational athletes. More than half of the league's participants resided in downtown Dayton, Ohio. We had built in an evangelistic element to the program, praying before each game and sharing the Gospel during halftimes. As the players, referees, and volunteer staff rehydrated from the contents of the five-gallon Gatorade cooler provided, we would share each week for two months the love of Jesus. Many came to faith in Christ.

During the earliest games of one particular season, I had gotten a call from my family that my grandpa and grandma were in a car accident. They had been hit by a drunk driver. My grandmother was killed. Grandpa was driving and was taken to the hospital with an injured leg as well as some broken ribs but would recover. At the time I received the news, I was not certain my grandpa was even aware yet that he had lost his wife. Neither of them knew the Lord. I have always hoped Grandma called on the name of Jesus in her final moments.

Two weeks prior to receiving that news, I had called Mom to share something weighing on my heart. I knew our family lived out the Gospel in front of my grandparents. They had prayed over meals, invited them to special Christmas services, would mail cards with inspirational Scriptures, and had faith-centered conversations when "appropriate." But *I* had never told them about Jesus and how He had personally forgiven *my* sins. The Holy Spirit was leading *me* to share the Gospel with my grandparents. Mom informed me that she had recently received a letter from Grandma, communicating their respect for our family's faith but clearly requesting none of us push the matter on either of them. I heeded my mother's caution instead of obeying the Holy Spirit's leading. When Grandma died, I was too late.

Grandpa was soon alone in his Kentucky home with his guilt. He had lost his best friend, his life's love, his bride. He couldn't help but feel responsible for her death since he was driving. It was not his fault. It was that drunk driver. I can't fathom Grandpa's feelings toward him. I had mixed emotions myself. He was put in prison. That is what needed to happen. Part of me wanted to go find the guy and punch him in the face. Another part of me wanted to share the Gospel with him. At one time, *I was him*. God forgave me. God could forgive him. Could I forgive him? Could Grandpa forgive him? Could Grandpa forgive himself? What a broken, sin-cursed world we live in.

After traveling back home from an out-of-state funeral, with tearful emotion, I shared with the men at basketball all that had transpired in our family. My passion for the Gospel grew exponentially, and I *pleaded* with the athletes in the room to trust Jesus while they still had time. No matter what their past, God would forgive them, and they could start over with a clean slate. Later that evening, when the games ended and nearly all had left, I had the awesome privilege to lead a young man from downtown, with a newborn son, to Christ. He wanted to leave his life of drug addiction and raise his son right, newly forgiven by Jesus. He and his family started attending our church, as he continued to participate in our sports evangelism programs. He would share his own personal testimony during future games, bringing others to the saving knowledge of Jesus Christ. God used Grandma's death to bring many to eternal life in Him.

Erin and I decided that any near future vacation plans would be on hold, and we were headed to visit Grandpa in Kentucky. We had a great time together hiking the Mammoth Caves and touring the Corvette Museum. Grandpa had more energy than I think we did. Even just visiting his home was delightful, getting to see his collection of model trains and reminiscing over years of family memories. During dinner out, I shared the Gospel with Grandpa. I laid it out for him similar to how I have in Scene 6 in this book.

We all cried as we expressed our love for one another, and I could tell the Lord was tugging at his heart. Grandpa did not trust Jesus that day. I am sure it was difficult to place faith in the truth Grandma had not. But he heard from me, read from Scripture himself, and knew God's redemptive plan for our brokenness. When I asked him what was keeping him from placing his faith in Jesus, he simply responded in tears, "God can't forgive me." I have never forgotten that.

Mom thought maybe it had something to do with his past military career. I speculated his response was at least in part due to the heavy misplaced guilt of Grandma's death. I suppose I will never fully know why he felt so unforgivable. Whatever was going on in his heart, God could certainly forgive it. Grandpa couldn't. Not yet. I told him I would be praying for him every day to place his trust in Jesus as Lord and Savior. For years, every time we spoke, I ended each conversation reminding him I was still praying for his salvation.

God is all about forgiveness. That is why He sent Jesus to die on a cross in our place so that our sins *could* be forgiven (*Heb. 9:22*). He loves to forgive, and it is the only solution for the brokenness all around us. Without forgiveness, unity would not exist in the church or in a family. For those a part of the body of Christ, forgiveness is a must. It is required. Vengeance belongs only to the Lord (*Rom. 12:19*), and yet He is still a God of great mercy, grace, love, and forgiveness.

The Exception

...Previously

Joseph went through the muck. He was mistreated, physically abused by family, sold into slavery as if he had no value, lied about, innocently imprisoned, and forgotten. He went through a lot. And in *Genesis 45*, he had the greatest opportunity for revenge.

Joseph started one day in jail and laid his head down that night on a palace pillow. Pharaoh had raised him to the position of "vice president" of Egypt. Still giving God the glory, he was able to interpret the dreams that shook Pharaoh to his core. Joseph warned him of unthinkable famine and became the project manager over Egypt's reserve grain storage during the years of plenty. Egypt was rescued from starvation during seven years of severe famine, along with many people groups from surrounding territories and all over, who were able to travel to Egypt to buy food. (*Gen. 41:14–57*)

Joseph was sold into slavery by his brothers at the age of seventeen. In his thirties, robed with royal Egyptian apparel, using an interpreter while speaking a different language, his brothers came to him for help so that their families would not starve to death. He recognized them, but they had no clue who it was they were requesting assistance from. He toyed with his brothers, testing them again and again, a crafty "cat-and-mouse" game. Joseph hid his secret overwhelming emotion very well. It was all for the purpose of seeing his younger brother, Benjamin, and his father again, for the purpose of restoring relationship with the entire family, for the purpose of saving their lives, and for the purpose of bringing God glory. (*Gen. 42–44*)

Joseph had all the power and all the leverage he needed to make his ten older brothers *pay* for what they did to him. He was in a position to rectify all he had gone through in his life because of them. Revenge would have tasted sweet and been totally justifiable. Under all the same circumstances, most people would at least be tempted to not pass up the opportunity. Joseph was the *exception*. He was a godly man, remaining faithful to the Lord, and his forgiveness was truly exceptional. I want to be like Joseph.

> *Then Joseph could not refrain himself before all them that stood by him; and he cried, Cause every man to go out from me. And there stood no man with him, while Joseph made himself known unto his brethren.*
>
> *And he wept aloud: and the Egyptians and the house of Pharaoh heard. And Joseph said unto his brethren, I am Joseph; doth my father yet live? And his brethren could not answer him; for they were troubled at his presence.*
>
> *And Joseph said unto his brethren, Come near to me, I pray you. And they came near. And he said, I am Joseph your brother, whom ye sold into Egypt.*
>
> *Now therefore be not grieved, nor angry with yourselves, that ye sold me hither: for God did send me before you to preserve life.*
>
> *For these two years hath the famine been in the land: and yet there are five years, in the which there shall neither be earing nor harvest.*
>
> *And God sent me before you to preserve you a posterity in the earth, and to save your lives by a great deliverance.*
>
> *So now it was not you that sent me hither, but God: and he hath made me a father to Pharaoh, and lord of all his house, and a ruler throughout all the land of Egypt.*

> *Haste ye, and go up to my father, and say unto him, Thus saith thy son Joseph, God hath made me lord of all Egypt: come down unto me, tarry not:*
>
> *and thou shalt dwell in the land of Goshen, and thou shalt be near unto me, thou, and thy children, and thy children's children, and thy flocks, and thy herds, and all that thou hast:*
>
> *and there will I nourish thee; for yet there are five years of famine; lest thou, and thy household, and all that thou hast, come to poverty.*
>
> *And, behold, your eyes see, and the eyes of my brother Benjamin, that it is my mouth that speaketh unto you.*
>
> *And ye shall tell my father of all my glory in Egypt, and of all that ye have seen; and ye shall haste and bring down my father hither.*
>
> *And he fell upon his brother Benjamin's neck, and wept; and Benjamin wept upon his neck.*
>
> *Moreover he kissed all his brethren, and wept upon them: and after that his brethren talked with him.*
>
> *And the <u>fame</u> thereof was heard in Pharaoh's house, saying, Joseph's brethren are come: and it pleased Pharaoh well, and his servants. (Gen. 45:1–16 KJV)*

I love how the King James Version reads, highlighted above in *verse 16*, that word *fame*. It could be said that as believers, our primary job as the church is to make the name of Jesus *famous*. I want to be a part of a local church body that people *know* forgives—a place where visitors enter the doors and the Holy Spirit's presence is evident. A family full of people who love Jesus and others, who don't judge, fight, or bicker but are *famous* for their unity and Christ-like forgiveness.

Joseph's brothers were done with him so many years before. He could have been done with them at that moment. He could have ended them. Instead, he embraced them, cried with them, brought them into a flourishing land, and provided for them and their little ones. Joseph showed great kindness, motivated by the faith he had all along that God was in complete control and had a purpose and a plan for his life. Joseph showed the love and forgiveness of Jesus.

> *"But as for you, ye thought evil against me; but God meant it unto good, to bring to pass, as it is this day, to save much people alive." (Gen. 50:20 KJV)*

The Expectation

Then Peter came up and said to him, "Lord, how often will my brother sin against me, and I forgive him? As many as seven times?" Jesus said to him, "I do not say to you seven times, but seventy-seven times." (Matt. 18:21–22 ESV)

The King James Version reads "seventy times seven." Do you know anyone who has sinned against you with the same repeated offense, let alone in completely different ways, *four hundred and ninety* times? I sure don't. How about *seventy-seven* times? Nope, me neither. Jesus was not being literal here. His response was intentionally quite "over the top." There is no limit to forgiveness. It is endless for Jesus, and the *expectation* is that it be endless for the Christ follower as well.

I do not know this with confidence, but I think there is enough reason to make a connection between this dialogue in *Matthew 18* and the dialogues that occurred in *Genesis 4.* As Jews, both Peter and Jesus would have Old Testament knowledge and even more specifically, have studied the Torah (the Law), *Genesis–Deuteronomy.*

> *Cain said to the Lord, "My punishment is greater than I can bear. Behold, you have driven me today away from the ground, and from your face I shall be hidden. I shall be a fugitive and a wanderer on the earth, and whoever finds me will kill me." Then the Lord said to him, "Not so! If anyone kills Cain, vengeance shall be taken on him sevenfold."*

And the Lord put a mark on Cain, lest any who found him should attack him. (Gen. 4:13–15 ESV)

God declared punishment *seven* times greater on anyone who would dare take Cain's life, because he killed his brother, Abel. Lamech, a distant relative to Cain, generations later made his own self-proclamation to his wives that punishment to anyone who would kill him would be greater *seventy-sevenfold.*

> *Lamech said to his wives: "Adah and Zillah, hear my voice; you wives of Lamech, listen to what I say: I have killed a man for wounding me, a young man for striking me. If Cain's revenge is sevenfold, then Lamech's is seventy-sevenfold." (Gen. 4:23–24 ESV)*

Both of these recorded events occurred because of the wickedness of murder. We see the same numbers (*seven and seventy-seven times*) being used by Peter and Jesus, not because of wickedness or punishment but to ask about and explain God's clear expectation of forgiveness. Jesus tells a parable to explain even further.

> *"Therefore the kingdom of heaven may be compared to a king who wished to settle accounts with his servants. When he began to settle, one was brought to him who owed him ten thousand talents. And since he could not pay, his master ordered him to be sold, with his wife and children and all that he had, and payment to be made. So the servant fell on his knees, imploring him, 'Have patience with me, and I will pay you everything.' And out of pity for him, the master of that servant released him and forgave him the debt. But when that same servant went out, he found one of his fellow servants who owed him a hundred denarii, and seizing him, he began to choke him, saying, 'Pay what you owe.' So*

his fellow servant fell down and pleaded with him, 'Have patience with me, and I will pay you.' He refused and went and put him in prison until he should pay the debt. When his fellow servants saw what had taken place, they were greatly distressed, and they went and reported to their master all that had taken place. Then his master summoned him and said to him, 'You wicked servant! I forgave you all that debt because you pleaded with me. And should not you have had mercy on your fellow servant, as I had mercy on you?' And in anger his master delivered him to the jailers, until he should pay all his debt. So also my heavenly Father will do to every one of you, if you do not forgive your brother from your heart." (Matt. 18:23–35 ESV)

Please don't miss the highlighted tail end of that passage, *verse 35*. When we talk about expectation, I implore you not to put any pastor, church leader, spiritual mentor, or anyone really on a pedestal at all. Do not set your expectations so high that they are impossible to reach. Each of us are broken, sin-cursed people, and in need of a Savior. It breaks my heart that this is a reality, but if you were to know me and spend any real amount of time around me, I would eventually in some way not meet your expectations. How do I know that? Because I am a sinner. And you are a sinner. And I learned long ago in ministry, when you put sinners in a room together, expect them to act like sinners. That is why forgiveness is so crucial for the believer desiring to honor Christ, for unity, and for God to bless a local church committed to reaching its community with the Gospel.

Our Example

Early in the morning he came again to the temple. All the people came to him, and he sat down and taught them. The scribes and the Pharisees brought a woman who had been caught in adultery, and placing her in the midst they said to him, "Teacher, this woman has been caught in the act of adultery. Now in the Law, Moses commanded us to stone such women. So what do you say?" This they said to test him, that they might have some charge to bring against him. Jesus bent down and wrote with his finger on the ground. And as they continued to ask him, he stood up and said to them, "Let him who is without sin among you be the first to throw a stone at her." And once more he bent down and wrote on the ground. But when they heard it, they went away one by one, beginning with the older ones, and Jesus was left alone with the woman standing before him. Jesus stood up and said to her, "Woman, where are they? Has no one condemned you?" She said, "No one, Lord." And Jesus said, "Neither do I condemn you; go, and from now on sin no more." (John 8:2–11 ESV)

I have always wondered what Jesus was writing. Were they actual words? Did anyone get a glimpse at it? Was He just drawing in the dirt? The Bible doesn't tell us. But one thing is for sure. My Savior is not easily shaken. He was so calm and collected. In the midst of their rushed attempt to catch Him off guard and get Him to slip with His response to their questions, He was as cool as a cucumber.

There was only one person present qualified to forgive sins. There was only one who was sinless, able to pick up a stone in response to what Jesus said, and that was Jesus Himself. Only He could condemn her. He chose forgiveness.

Jesus is our *example*. His entire life and ministry surrounded the theme of forgiveness. His last moments before He died were all about forgiveness. Even nailed to the cross, He was forgiving the criminal being crucified next to Him (*Luke 23:43*). I don't understand His kind of love. I know my own sin, and I believe Jesus would have laid down His life if He saved only me. But to think of the sins of the entire human race, past, present, and future; to think of the ones there, spitting at Him, tearing His beard out from the roots, pressing the crown of thorns deep into His scalp, and those literally driving the nails into His flesh; and to think as He was suffocating, how He struggled, pushing up on those nails just to catch a breath so He could pray the words, "Father, forgive them" (*Luke 23:34*). I don't understand that kind of love. But I want so desperately to follow Christ's example.

Unforgivable?

We have all been on both broken sides of conflict to some degree and at some point in our lives. Perhaps, the offense was against us. Maybe we were the one who wronged someone else. It could have been avoided if we didn't lack wisdom at times. It is possible it was completely on purpose and a totally selfish act. How do we rebuild those burned bridges? How do we regain trust? How do we forgive ourselves when we have totally screwed up? How do we forgive someone else's offense that seems absolutely unforgivable? "I can't make it right, because they won't even talk to me." "You don't know what they did." "They haven't come and asked for forgiveness."

I pastored at a church that had a drinking fountain that was "possessed." I figured it out the hard way the first week I was on staff there. I bent down to get a drink, and after a few seconds, the flow of water changed and shot me in the eye. I quickly gave up on that option and began filling my water bottle instead. But from time to time, the water pressure would change so drastically that the fountain would shoot over my water bottle, past its own drain, only to land on the floor. It always made a mess on the carpet. You needed a bucket for the overflow.

You know, Jesus is the same way. The overflow of His forgiveness is endless. How He has forgiven each of us in our sins, paying our penalty in our place, in complete innocence, when we focus on that, suddenly forgiving someone else for the most difficult offense becomes easier to do. Those who are forgiven much are able to forgive much. When forgiveness seems impossible, get yourself a bucket, and draw from the fountain that is Christ and His overflow of end-less forgiveness (*Eph. 4:32*).

Pray. Pray for God to help rebuild those burned bridges. Pray that God would help you be a person who is loyal and trustworthy. Pray that God would help you draw from His endless forgiveness to forgive others and yes, to forgive even yourself. If repentance is needed, search for every way possible without hesitation to seek forgiveness. If another does not repent, forgive from your heart anyway. Give it to God, and let it go. As the Lord allows you to cross paths, in a spirit of forgiveness, pursue restored relationships in Christ's love. Never forget how much you have been forgiven by a perfect, holy, righteous, sinless Savior.

What Are You Waiting For?

The Lord had graced Grandpa many additional years after that deadly car accident. He got to witness many of his great grandchildren grow, and others come into the world and join our family. Many more holidays were celebrated and meals shared. Many more memories were made and there were many more opportunities to say yes to Jesus.

At a very old age, Grandpa's health began to decline. God had graced him those additional years, but no one can live forever. Even the healthiest body will eventually breakdown. I would receive reports on how he was doing from Mom on the phone from a distance. She would get information from her sisters there with Grandpa in Kentucky. Eventually, doctors would let our family know it was only a matter of days until he would pass.

One of my aunts in Kentucky would talk with me often through social media instant messenger. She would provide updates on Grandpa's health, as well as conversations she would have with Mom during Grandpa's final days. As we grew closer during those sad moments, I came to find out she was not only my aunt but my sister in Christ as well. She had come to faith in Jesus some time during those years after the accident. It was wonderful news. Our conversations quickly turned from Grandpa's physical ailments to his spiritual eternity. My aunt concisely asked, "Has anyone shared with Dad yet how he can be saved?" Of course, I called Mom immediately to share the good news about her sister, as well as to encourage her to call Grandpa and have a Gospel conversation with him.

I don't think Mom would consider her spiritual gift evangelism. She urged me to call Grandpa and share the Gospel with him again.

I felt there was wisdom in further encouraging my mother to make the call instead. "Mom, there is nothing I can say to him that I have not said already. You need to be the one to do this. He is dying. There is nothing to fear. Not rejection. Not saying the wrong words or not being able to answer any possible questions. He is literally drowning in his sin, about to enter an eternity apart from Jesus, and you have a rescue boat. You have the Gospel. Jesus wants to save him. What are you waiting for?" I prayed with her. As we hung up, I eagerly waited for the phone to ring again, as I continued to pray the Holy Spirit would get a hold of my grandfather's heart. A couple of hours later, Mom called me back in excitement with joyful tears.

Four days before my grandpa passed away, he had called on the name above all names, Jesus. Mom had led him to Christ over the phone. What a wonderful miracle for a daughter to experience and participate in with her father. I believe (in part), God rescued my mom physically from her stroke so He could rescue her dad spiritually years later. Grandpa trusted Jesus as his personal Lord and Savior. His faith became his sight—a citizen of Heaven, a child of God, forever forgiven. Praise the Lord!

I was so honored to officiate Grandpa's funeral. The Gospel was preached. I shared Grandpa's story and how he had come to faith in Christ. Several in attendance responded to the message, trusting in Jesus as well. Those folks left the service that day, new in Christ, having also experienced His endless forgiveness.

SCENE 5

Smells Like Fish

Our family has been richly blessed by the years and the ministries the Lord has allowed us platforms to serve Him. I am still amazed at how God could use someone like me in any way to see souls saved and lives forever changed. I am not "a Paul." I am not "a Doctor Luke." I never have been. I'm "a Peter." I am a "smelly fisherman." And I am so thankful God uses smelly fishermen to advance His Kingdom, to bring Himself glory and to reach the world with the Gospel.

I have a lot in common with Peter. I am nothing special in and of myself. Not incredibly gifted to speak of. Kind of a blue collar, "every man." Hard working, with a very hands-on approach. Not highly educated. Not incredibly wealthy. Passionate, headstrong, and I can be a fierce friend. Very relational. A leader, but at times can quickly start "chewing on my sneaker."

When my will is broken before the Lord, and I am completely surrendered to His will, that is when the Holy Spirit can show up and show off. That is when God can use me in ways I have never imagined. Josh is a nobody, not impressive at all. But Josh plus Christ, led by Christ, obedient to Christ, wholeheartedly serving Christ, there is nothing the Lord cannot do with that heart. The world can be turned upside down for Jesus.

92

Called

In *Matthew 4*, after the record of Christ's forty-day fast and Satan's attempt to break Him through temptations, just before the sermon on the mount when Jesus unpacked the beatitudes in *chapter 5*, we see His first encounter with the disciple, Peter. At the earliest parts of Christ's three-year ministry prior to His crucifixion, Peter embarked on a new life adventure, becoming one of Jesus' closest friends and partners in Kingdom work.

> *From that time Jesus began to preach, saying, "Repent, for the kingdom of heaven is at hand."*
> *While walking by the Sea of Galilee, he saw two brothers, Simon (who is called Peter) and Andrew his brother, casting a net into the sea, for they were fishermen. And he said to them, "Follow me, and I will make you fishers of men." Immediately they left their nets and followed him. (Matt. 4:17–20 ESV)*

If all of us reading this book were to collectively put our heads together, we could definitely come up with some facts about Peter. One thing we know for sure, Peter knew fish. He was a fisherman. He would catch the fish. He would net the fish. He would get the fish. He would cut the fish. He would gut the fish. He would cook the fish. He would eat the fish. He would sell the fish. And He smelled like fish every day of his life. Being a fisherman was a good job, especially at that time and in that culture. It was important. It had value. But Jesus had a job for Peter to do that had eternal value.

Christ met Peter right where he was at, and He made it *real* for him. Requesting that he lay down his nets and forsake all that he knew, Jesus told Peter, "*Follow me, and I will make you a fisher of men.*" Peter was *CALLED* to the Gospel ministry.

If you are a follower of Christ, you are called to the Gospel ministry. Not all of us are called to serve the same way. Not everyone is called to be a pastor or to be a missionary. Most are not called to author a book on practical Christian living. We don't all have the same spiritual gifts and talents. Not everyone has the gift of hospitality or the gift of encouragement. Not everyone has the spiritual gift of evangelism. But let me say this, as Christians, we are *all* called to evangelize. If nothing else, we all have our own story of how Christ redeemed us, in our brokenness, and we need to share that story with the world (*Acts 1:8*).

I have spent half of my life serving in the local church, encouraging, equipping, and training those a part of the body of Christ on how to share their faith (*Eph. 4:12*). I have strived to instill in students not to be afraid of rejection or to not have all the answers to possible questions when sharing the Gospel. It's okay to say, "I don't know," or "I'll get back to you on that." It's not wrong to not have all the answers, but it is wrong to never open your mouth and tell others about Jesus. I have been saved now for twenty-nine years. And if in that time frame, I were to not have shared the Gospel even once, I'd have a real problem. I would need to reevaluate my relationship with the Lord in the midst of my disobedience. I cannot just be *content to know*. The Lord has commissioned *me* to make disciples (*Matt. 28:19*). I want to be willing to do whatever it takes to get people in front of the Gospel.

I once led a group of students and adult leaders on a mission trip to New York City. The youngest able to participate that summer were the eighth-grade students entering their freshman year of high school in the fall. On our team was a young lady (*Let's call her Penny.*) that had just met the age requirement. Though she was going to be a freshman, she looked like she could have just graduated sixth grade. She was very small in stature and had a quiet, timid personality to match her physical appearance. Penny was not outgoing or spiritually self-motivated. She had not demonstrated any defining leadership qualities and in fear, would often "attach herself to Pastor Josh's hip" as the team would serve.

We partnered with a mission organization and downtown church ministry, and at the heart of this trip was evangelism. We would spend each day for over a week sharing the Gospel everywhere we could go in the city and with everyone we encountered. That might have meant a conversation on the basketball courts or soccer fields. It could have been people we met in the park or a two-minute conversation on the subway before someone reached their stop. Bible lessons were taught during outdoor community vacation Bible school-type programming. We trained quite a bit before and even while on the trip, how to share our faith in all kinds of unique scenarios. There were many different teams serving the Kingdom on mission that week in the same ways, but the Gospel outreach that took place within just our team transformed my life and ministry.

About halfway through our trip, our group visited Central Park. There were hundreds of people there that day, exercising, playing sports, throwing frisbees, or just getting some sun. We prayed the Lord would go before us, as we broke up into smaller groups of three or four to spread out and cover all the territory. I decided to let Penny and the other young ladies in her group go on without me that time, hopeful they would step out of their comfort zones. I observed from a distance, as I kept a watchful eye on all the students on our team. Moments later, I discovered Penny, and the rest of her group, literally hiding behind a tree. They were terrified. I knew I had to say something.

I called a "holy huddle."

"Girls, come here, bring it in! Are you afraid? Penny, are you afraid to share your faith?"

"Pastor Josh, I am so scared."

"Girls, look across the park. Look at the hundreds that are here today. It is a great probability that the majority of these people are not saved. We have to allow the Holy Spirit to change our hearts, give us courage, make us passionate for the Gospel, and have great compassion

for the lost. I want you to imagine that we have information no one else here does. We have received intel that there is a bomb headed to Central Park, and we are all going to die in five minutes. Most of these folks are going to enter into eternity apart from Christ, in a very real place the Bible calls Hell. You have what they need. You have the Gospel of Jesus Christ. Penny, what do you want to do?"

I saw a tear leave her eye as that little girl rose up and became a *GIANT.*

"Pastor Josh, I want to gather all these people together and scream at the top of my lungs, 'Listen, everyone! There is a bomb on the way, and we are all going to die in five minutes. I *need* to tell you about Jesus.'" I am not kidding. Within five minutes, Penny and those other girls led a stranger, a middle-aged man, to Christ. I had never seen anything like it. If Penny can do it, then you and I can do it. Amen? It is God who brings the increase. He goes before us and prepares the heart of an individual to respond to the truth of the Gospel. He brings people to Himself. He saves. All we have to do is open our mouths and say the words (*Rom. 10:14–15*).

Changed

Peter was a part of one of the Bible's first recorded "small groups." I have always felt that I followed in Jesus' footsteps, as He too led a "student ministry." Please, understand that Christ's twelve disciples got to do life with Him, serve with Him, and experience firsthand His many miracles.

Peter saw Lazarus raised from the dead (*John 11:43–44*). He knew with confidence, with a spoken word, a simple touch, just a thought by Jesus, the leper could be healed (*Matt. 8:2–3*). Peter witnessed Jesus' power demonstrated as He calmed the storm (*Mark 4:38–39*). He had never seen that before. Peter was rescued from drowning, as he reached up and grabbed the Savior's hand, while Jesus' feet were firmly planted on the surface of the water, defying gravity (*Matt. 14:28–32*). Peter, along with the rest of the disciples, knew that Jesus was different. He was special. God's hand and blessing were on the man and His ministry.

> *He said to them, "But who do you say that I am?" Simon Peter replied, "You are the Christ, the Son of the living God." (Matt 16: 15–16 ESV)*

I believe the disciples thought that Jesus was going to take the throne then and there. They were hopeful that His reign in their physical kingdom on Earth would relieve them of Roman rule and oppression. As Jesus' closest friends, that would have worked out well for them. They would have continued to serve by His side, as valuable high-level palace leaders. Their anticipation and understanding fell short of Christ's Heavenly purposes.

Jesus tried to tell the disciples of His necessary path to the cross. They just didn't get it yet. How could the Messiah, their King, rule and deliver them from the Romans, if He was to be brutally crucified? That didn't register. He had power that was unmatched. Surely, He could not be defeated.

We know Judas Iscariot betrayed Jesus. The other eleven disciples would crumble in terror at Jesus' capture. When Peter's confidence level was super high, he led the men in proclamation that he would not only never abandon Christ, but he would in fact lay down his life for Him before he would ever deny Him. It was a real *"no way, José"* response. I believe when Peter spoke those words, he was genuine. The problem wasn't his sincerity. It was that he still didn't fully understand why Jesus had come.

> *And when they had sung a hymn, they went out to the Mount of Olives. Then Jesus said to them, "You will all fall away because of me this night. For it is written, 'I will strike the shepherd, and the sheep of the flock will be scattered.' But after I am raised up, I will go before you to Galilee." Peter answered him, "Though they all fall away because of you, I will never fall away." Jesus said to him, "Truly, I tell you, this very night, before the rooster crows, you will deny me three times." Peter said to him, "Even if I must die with you, I will not deny you!" And all the disciples said the same. (Matt. 26:30–35 ESV)*

Can you relate to Peter the way I can? Do you ever rely on yourself, your own strength and ability, trying to *perform* in your own understanding? Have you ever strived to serve the Lord, while at the same time eliminating Him from the process? When I don't let the Holy Spirit lead me, I always fall flat on my face. Success happens when I am seeking Christ, and He is guiding and directing my steps. (*Prov. 3:5–6*)

As Judas led the soldiers to locate Jesus and the other disciples in the garden, the moment for Peter to prove himself faithful to protect Christ arrived. He really rose to the occasion at Jesus' arrest. I don't know if it was a knife or a sword as we would think of it, but it was definitely a blade. I'm not sure if he was trying to kill the guy or if he just had bad aim, but as a self-appointed secret service agent for the Lord, Peter cut off the ear of Malchus. He ran toward the danger, proving himself faithful. (*John 18:3–10*)

Then Jesus did something that confused the disciples more than ever before. It messed them up. Jesus didn't need protection. He didn't need Peter to "have His back." The Lord put his hand on the side of Malchus' head and healed his ear (*Luke 22:51*). Then He willingly surrendered himself (*John 10:18*). The Bible doesn't say this, but I have always liked the thought of Malchus trusting Jesus as Lord and Savior after the events of that night. I would imagine he at least questioned in his heart whether or not it was right to apprehend Christ.

Peter and the rest of the disciples were scratching their heads wondering what was happening. Jesus had been betrayed by one of *them* in their inner circle. They would soon experience an incredible identity crisis. They must have wondered why Jesus wasn't doing anything. Why wasn't He taking this opportunity to rise to the throne? Their confidence levels instantly dropped to an all-time low. Fear and doubt took over. They scattered and ran, terrified (*Mark 14:50*). Soon, Peter would be so consumed with protecting himself from danger, he'd have no clue that he was fulfilling Christ's earlier prophecy of his denial. Probably the Bible's worst broken promise ever made directly to the Son of God.

> *Simon Peter followed Jesus, and so did another disciple. Since that disciple was known to the high priest, he entered with Jesus into the courtyard of the high priest, but Peter stood outside at the door. So the other disciple, who was known to the high priest, went out and spoke to the servant girl who kept watch at the door, and brought Peter in. The*

servant girl at the door said to Peter, "You also are not one of this man's disciples, are you?" He said, "I am not." Now the servants and officers had made a charcoal fire, because it was cold, and they were standing and warming themselves. Peter also was with them, standing and warming himself. (John 18:15–18 ESV)

Now Simon Peter was standing and warming himself. So they said to him, "You also are not one of his disciples, are you?" He denied it and said, "I am not." One of the servants of the high priest, a relative of the man whose ear Peter had cut off, asked, "Did I not see you in the garden with him?" Peter again denied it, and at once a rooster crowed. (John 18:25–27 ESV)

Strike one, he denied Christ. Strike two, he denied Christ. Strike three, Peter didn't have "a leg to stand on." *Cock-a-doodle-doo!* Let me tell you, if someone cut off the ear of my wife or one of my kids and I was there, and then I saw them again, I would recognize the man. Peter was "running" the opposite direction, away from the danger, trying to save his own neck. Lying straight through his teeth, he was looking out for *numero uno.* Jesus was no longer his priority.

Have you ever been unfaithful to the Lord or broken a promise you vowed to Him? Have you failed God in any way that brought you the overwhelming shame and guilt Peter must have felt the moment he heard that rooster and remembered Jesus' prophetic words? How can we *fail forward* when we have broken our relationship with Christ so deeply? Remember, His faithfulness is not contingent on our faithfulness. *He* is the reason we even have a relationship with Him, not us. If we can trust Him for our eternity, then we can trust Him for our today. No greater forgiveness is found in any other than Jesus. Confess your sin. Repent. He will be faithful to forgive each and every time (*1 John 1:9*).

After His resurrection, Jesus had revealed Himself to the disciples for the third time, preparing breakfast for them on the seashore, after they had brought in a large haul of fish. This was so familiar to all of them. It was easy for the disciples to return to what they knew before their three-year ministry serving alongside Christ. I am sure Peter felt *broken* and no longer *usable* in the Gospel ministry, but nothing was further from the truth. Jesus took the time to speak with Peter one-on-one, reaffirming God's plan and purpose for his life.

When they got out on land, they saw a charcoal fire in place, with fish laid out on it, and bread. Jesus said to them, "Bring some of the fish that you have just caught." So Simon Peter went aboard and hauled the net ashore, full of large fish, 153 of them. And although there were so many, the net was not torn. Jesus said to them, "Come and have breakfast." Now none of the disciples dared ask him, "Who are you?" They knew it was the Lord. Jesus came and took the bread and gave it to them, and so with the fish. This was now the third time that Jesus was revealed to the disciples after he was raised from the dead.

When they had finished breakfast, Jesus said to Simon Peter, "Simon, son of John, do you love me more than these?" He said to him, "Yes, Lord; you know that I love you." He said to him, "Feed my lambs." He said to him a second time, "Simon, son of John, do you love me?" He said to him, "Yes, Lord; you know that I love you." He said to him, "Tend my sheep." He said to him the third time, "Simon, son of John, do you love me?" Peter was grieved because he said to him the third time, "Do you love me?" and he said to him, "Lord, you know everything; you know that I love you." Jesus said to him, "Feed my sheep. Truly, truly, I say to you, when you were young, you used to dress yourself and walk

*wherever you wanted, but when you are old, you
will stretch out your hands, and another will dress
you and carry you where you do not want to go."
(This he said to show by what kind of death he was
to glorify God.) And after saying this he said to him,*
"Follow me." (John 21:9–19 ESV)

I don't think it was an accident that Jesus asked about Peter's love for Him *three times*. His heart needed to be broken before the Lord (*Psalm 51:17*). Only Peter could be grieved over such a conversation, even after denying Christ repeatedly. Peter was right though, Jesus did know everything and his love for Him already. Peter was charged to "feed the Lord's sheep." He would be instrumental in the beginning of the church. Jesus revealed to Peter he would still have the opportunity to show himself faithful, even unto death. Christ prophesied once again this time that Peter would lay down his life for the cause of the Gospel. Church tradition tells us that Peter was also crucified but felt unworthy to die in the same manner as his Savior and so requested he be hung upside down. He was a martyr for Jesus, obedient to his original call to ministry, *following* Christ to the end of his life. Peter was *CHANGED*.

I have never been faced with the decision to give up my life for Jesus or to deny Him. In full transparency, that's a tough one. We are blessed in America with great freedoms still. The day may come in my lifetime when those freedoms no longer exist. As a pastor, a leader in local church ministry, I may have to make a life-threatening choice for the cause of the Gospel. I pray I will remain faithful to my Lord. How about you? Do you love Jesus? I won't ask three times. But are you willing to do whatever it takes to advance Christ's Kingdom and to see lost souls saved? Are you willing to give everything you have to offer to see the good news of the Gospel spread everywhere and to everyone?

What caused such a change in Peter and the rest of the disciples? What turned their fear into boldness? What stopped them from fleeing potential danger, redirecting them to running toward opportunities to fearlessly preach the Gospel, no matter what? The answer is, they saw Jesus raised from the dead. They finally understood. That change in the disciples, in Peter, is recorded evidence of the truth of the Bible.

Have you been changed by Jesus? If you call yourself a Christian, you should want to tell people about Christ. You should want to live your life in worshipful obedience, in a way that is pleasing to the Lord. If you believe you have been saved but know there has been no real change in your life, there is no better time for spiritual reevaluation than now. The Bible says that we become a new creature when God calls us to salvation in Jesus. Who we were has passed, and there is a change God is making in us. (*2 Cor. 5:17*) My prayer is that people who don't know the Lord in my circle of influence recognize something different in me and want to know what it is all about.

Church Grower

Peter was CALLED. Peter was CHANGED. And Peter was a CHURCH GROWER.

I've served in large churches as well as small churches, long-established churches, and new church plants. I've seen God bless them all. Numbers have never concerned me much, but every number is a life. Every life is a soul that can be transformed by Jesus. The number I care about most is "the next one," the next person God would allow me the privilege to lead to Christ and to disciple.

In the beginning of his church ministry, after Jesus' ascension to Heaven, Peter preached the Gospel without apology. Nothing would shut him up. Nothing would stop God's call on his life, and the change that took place in him brought masses to Christ's salvation. He would go on even to write part of the New Testament. Jesus was his priority. He finally got it. His focus was on God's eternal, Heavenly Kingdom. The church was not only beginning, it was growing with each passing day. The fact that God called me to be a pastor in local church ministry and that my family and I are able to worship regularly within our local body of believers is largely due to the pastoring, preaching, church planting, and church-growing Gospel ministry of Peter. He was a fisher of men.

"And it shall come to pass that everyone who calls upon the name of the Lord shall be saved.'
"Men of Israel, hear these words: Jesus of Nazareth, a man attested to you by God with mighty works and wonders and signs that God did through

him in your midst, as you yourselves know—this Jesus, delivered up according to the definite plan and foreknowledge of God, you crucified and killed by the hands of lawless men. God raised him up, loosing the pangs of death, because it was not possible for him to be held by it." (Acts 2:21–24 ESV)

"Let all the house of Israel therefore know for certain that God has made him both Lord and Christ, this Jesus whom you crucified." Now when they heard this they were cut to the heart, and said to Peter and the rest of the apostles, "Brothers, what shall we do?" And Peter said to them, "Repent and be baptized every one of you in the name of Jesus Christ for the forgiveness of your sins, and you will receive the gift of the Holy Spirit. For the promise is for you and for your children and for all who are far off, everyone whom the Lord our God calls to himself." And with many other words he bore witness and continued to exhort them, saying, "Save yourselves from this crooked generation." So those who received his word were baptized, and there were added that day about three thousand souls.

And they devoted themselves to the apostles' teaching and the fellowship, to the breaking of bread and the prayers. And awe came upon every soul, and many wonders and signs were being done through the apostles. And all who believed were together and had all things in common. And they were selling their possessions and belongings and distributing the proceeds to all, as any had need. And day by day, attending the temple together and breaking bread in their homes, they received their food with glad and generous hearts, praising God and having favor with all the people. And the Lord added to their number day by day those who were being saved. (Acts 2:36–47 ESV)

I don't know what God has for me in the near future. I don't know how He will use our family or what He will do through our church. I have no idea how He may bless this book. What I do know is that, the Lord can do anything He wants, and by His grace, I will remain faithful in serving Him with all I have to offer.

I don't believe there is any higher calling on this earth, during the time God gives us in this life, than to point as many people to Jesus as possible. There are only two things in our existence that are eternal, God's Word and the human soul. I want what matters most to matter most in my life. I want to spend as much time as I can investing in eternity.

If God is in control, reaching more than three thousand souls in the months and years ahead is certainly an attainable goal. I am just a "smelly fisherman," and I am so incredibly grateful God uses smelly fishermen to advance His Kingdom, to bring Himself glory, and to reach the world with the good news of the Gospel.

SCENE 6

Personal Evangelism

This next section is a reminder to the believer in Christ of the undeserving, amazing grace in which we live daily, and I hope never becomes stale to any of us. As you read on, I pray the Gospel truth within these words remains fresh, and our salvation found in Jesus' shed blood on Calvary's cross is more precious to us today than the moment we first placed our faith and trust in Him.

For the reader who has yet to say yes to Jesus, this is the greatest news you will ever hear. Please, consider Jesus today (*2 Cor. 6:2*). Read all the way to the end. Bring your BIG questions to God, and ask Him to reveal Himself to you. He will (*Jer. 29:13*). Read from His Word the Lord's beautiful redemptive plan for our brokenness. He will use you. God is not confusing. Jesus loves you and *wants* you. Listen intently to the Holy Spirit speaking to your heart. He has a plan and a purpose for *your* life.

The following is a demonstration and example of my own personal Gospel presentation. For years, I have applied this to large and smaller group-speaking engagements, as well as one-on-one individual conversations. The illustrations may be modified from time to time, but the truth of the Scriptures used are unchangeable. This is training for the believer in how to share your faith. For the one seeking the Lord, this is the good news of the Gospel of Jesus Christ.

I would like to share with you a *fictional* story of a conversation I had with a new friend I met in the community of our church where we now serve. I say fictional because there have been hundreds of stories in the ministries God has called me to just like this one. So this is based on true events. Michael and I were in a restaurant having lunch. He knew I was a pastor and a man of faith. As our friendship grew, I knew he wanted to talk. There was some real brokenness in his life.

As I shared with Michael my heart, I asked him to read frequently from the pages of my own personal study Bible that I preach out of. I came prepared, having previously earmarked sections with specific verses highlighted for him. I believe God's Word spoken from Michael's own lips was most powerful. I would like to invite you into our conversation. **Michael's words are in bold print.** *My words are italicized.*

Two Questions

Hello, my friend! I am so glad we got the chance to connect over lunch today. How have you been?

Yah, me too! It's been a little while since we have been able to do this. Thanks for carving out the time in your schedule. I am doing okay, all things considered.

I have been praying for you, with everything that is going on in your life right now. If I can serve you in any other way, please don't hesitate to reach out.

Thank you. That means a lot to me. Just getting together to talk helps more than you may realize.

I'm so glad. Michael, you obviously know that I am a pastor, and I don't think it would surprise you if the direction of our conversation today went toward spiritual things. I have wanted to talk with you for quite some time now, about who I am in Christ, why I serve in ministry, and why we are even sitting here talking over lunch today. You are important to me. This is not an accident. Quite frankly, I have the best news you could ever hear, and you do not want to miss out. Would it be okay for me to share?

Pastor Josh, I am all ears!

Wonderful! You've probably already noticed my Bible here on the table. I am going to set it aside for now. I actually don't want to start with that. I want to ask you two questions. Whenever I share my faith with anyone, an individual or a crowd of people, I always ask these two questions first. (1) Do you believe in absolute truth? (2) Do you believe in intelligent design? We don't all come from the same family background or life experiences. I would be naive to assume we all "have stock" in the same faith system. The point is we are different. I believe these two questions can get everyone on an equal level playing field. So that's my goal. I want us to both start in the same place. What are your thoughts on question number one? Do you believe in absolute truth?

Well, I have to be honest. I am not even certain I fully understand what that means.

Thank you for that, Michael. Let me help clarify. Absolute truth, simply put, means ONE TRUTH. Do you see this Sweet' N Low packet here in the condiment caddy on our table? What color is it?

It's pink.

Really? I think it's green. What color is it?

It is most definitely pink.

Sorry, I REALLY BELIEVE it is green. So what color is it?

Without a shadow of a doubt, it is absolutely PINK!

You are confident it is pink, but I say it is green. Who's right?

I am.

Ha ha! Yah, you're right. It is pink. We both have eyes connected to brains that are capable of common sense thought, as well as the ability to grow in the understanding of simple observation and the recognition of basic colors. We're smart! We both know that is a pink packet of zero-calorie sugar substitute. Not a single guest in this restaurant would be foolish enough to stand up and publicly proclaim something as simple as that packet to be green. They would be embarrassed from all the laughter. We ALL know the absolute truth is that it is pink. But there are people all over the world willing to be equally foolish with a matter as important as their eternity. They will claim that you can believe what you believe, and they can believe whatever else it is that they believe. And the both of you will end up in the same place when you die someday. You see, we can both be right, or we can both be wrong. But there is only ONE absolute truth. I suppose I could be color-blind. But that doesn't change the truth of the packet being pink. Knowing my limitations in understanding that truth, due to my color blindness, I should explore other ways of discovering the absolute truth in regard to its color, including but not limited to having someone else (who knows the truth) inform me. I believe everyone believes in absolute truth. They just don't always admit it. So how about you, Michael? Do you believe in absolute truth?

I guess I do.

Yah, me too. How about that second question? Do you believe in intelligent design?

I might need your help explaining that one too.

Okay. I want you to imagine that you and I are getting away for a few days of much-needed vacation time. We can bring anyone along we would like. We are all going on a cruise. FUN! We're having a great time until horrible weather rolls in. The ship is hit with such a bad storm that our cruise liner capsizes and sinks, and everyone onboard is lost at sea except you. You are the only one still alive. As you wash up on the shore of an uninhabited island, you immediately go into survival mode. You need food, fresh water, and shelter. You grab a large stick and start whacking at the tall weed grass as your search begins. Suddenly, something from the ground nearly blinds you with the reflection of the sun. You realize it is a smartphone. The battery has died, so there is no chance of calling for help. But you are filled with hope, because what thought has taken over the moment?

Maybe someone else is here?

That is exactly right. Maybe I am not alone on this island. Maybe someone else is here. Or at least, someone else was here at some point. Maybe there is help. Anyone's mind would be immediately flooded with thoughts like these when in the same desperate situation. Why? Remember, Michael, human beings are smart. No one would ever assume that the protective case, the glass touch screen, the speaker and microphone, the flash bulb, as well as the camera lens, function buttons, and the battery inside all came together by chance, and POOF, there was a cell phone. There was intelligent design involved in the making of that product. It was created, sold, and purchased, and then brought to this location somehow.

No one in this restaurant would be foolish enough to publicly make the claim that that phone came into existence all on its own because of random chance. No one would deny that there was a superior, intelligent being involved somehow and at some point. But there are people all over the world putting their trust in evolutionary theory. Take the human body alone, for example. You are so much more intricate than a smartphone. Your bone structure. Your muscle tissue. The pigmentation of your skin and your hair. The retinas of your eyes. The DNA strands of your body's makeup. So much more complex than a phone, and yet people all over the world will claim you and I exist because of random chance. I believe everyone believes in intelligent design. They just don't always admit it. So I'll ask again. How about you, Michael? Do you believe in intelligent design?

Yes. I sure do.

I do too. Consider that sandwich on your plate. I am not super creative, but I think I could make a sandwich similar to the one you are eating for lunch. Could you imagine if I made a sandwich, and then that sandwich began to speak and tell me IT was the boss. What if that sandwich told me it was not happy with how I made it and then voiced strong opinions on its purpose and how it felt the rest of its existence should play out. Ludicrous, right? You and I agree on both absolute truth and intel-

ligent design. Michael, what that ultimately means is that we are not the designer but rather the designed. And as the designed, we lack authority and position to lay claim on absolute truth. Only the designer is able to establish standard rules and guidelines. As the designed, we should seek after the designer to find out what his expectations are for us. I would like to now read Scripture with you and propose that the God of the Bible is a reasonable, feasible solution to what it is we are talking about.

Okay. Let's do it.

A World Broken

In the beginning, God created the heavens and the earth. (Gen. 1:1 ESV)

God created. He created everything. He created the skies and the seas. The birds and the trees. The flowers and the bees. He created you and me. (Rom. 1:20) Do you know the names of the first people we see that God created in the Bible?

Adam and Eve, right?

You got it. God called all of His creation good, but mankind was most precious to Him. He did not need us. He didn't have to make us. He wanted us. God created us in His own image (Gen. 1:27), unique from all the rest of His creation, and it was always His desire to walk in close, intimate, relationship with man. In the newness of creation and existence, God only voiced one command for Adam (and Eve) to refrain from eating of the fruit from the tree of the knowledge of good and evil (Gen. 2:17). As a father, I have joked for years that the explanation "because I said so" is sufficient for my children. If it was good enough for God, it is good enough for me. Ha! The Bible doesn't tell us why Adam and Eve were not permitted to eat of that particular fruit. We just know that to do so would have been rebellion against the Creator. And that is exactly what happened. They rebelled, and as they ate the forbidden fruit in complete disobedience, sin entered into the world (Gen. 3:6).

God's creation was stained, and man's relationship with God was broken. The Lord is righteous, holy, pure, sinless, and perfect. He cannot have anything to do with sin. It was not God's fault, it was ours. We messed up. That broken, cancer-like sin nature "disease" has been passed down through every generation since the beginning. Adam and Eve's children were sinners. Their kids' kids and grandkids were sinners too. All the way down to my parents, me, and now my children. We all make mistakes. None of us are perfect (Rom. 3:10*). We are all part of this broken, sin-cursed world, undeserving of the relationship God created us to have with Him. I'd like you to read out loud, please, this verse in the New Testament book of Romans, and tell me what you think it means.*

For all have sinned and fall short of the glory of God… *(Rom. 3:23 ESV)*

Well, ALL means everyone. So it is definitely saying that everyone is a sinner against God.

Yes. Very good. That includes you and me. Let's imagine again that we are standing at the edge of the Grand Canyon. You, me, and an Olympic gold medalist holding the world record in the long jump. We are each going to take a turn, attempting to jump from one side of the canyon to the other. I will go first. I leap with all my strength and get pretty far for a large mammal who has had no training. But I end up falling straight to the bottom from an incredible height. I don't survive. You're up next. You are pretty athletic. You even get a bit of a running start. You end up jumping two times farther than I did. Impressive! But you join me at the bottom. Now, it is time for the Olympic athlete. He "smokes" both our efforts. Though he jumped incredibly farther than either of us, he still fell short of the other side of the canyon and joined us in a gruesome death. We don't measure ourselves against others, how good or bad we are compared to them. Scripture tells us that if you have broken one part of the law, you have broken it all (James 2:10*). God's perfection is the standard in which we are measured against, and every one of us falls short in the brokenness of our sin. Here is another verse I would like you to read. Tell me your thoughts.*

For the wages of sin is death, but the free gift of God is eternal life in Christ Jesus our Lord. *(Rom. 6:23 ESV)*

Correct me if I am wrong. It sounds like death is the direct result of our sin. And the second half of that verse has to have something to do with that good news you were talking about earlier. Right?

Right on the money, Bud. Speaking of money, we both have jobs and earn a salary or a wage. It has been a long time since I have been paid with an actual hard copy paycheck. Almost everyone operates through direct deposit these days. But I remember the excitement of my earliest employment as a teenager, earning minimum wage, opening my very first paycheck. How fast do you think that excitement would have left me if I read the payment balance and on the line was printed the word DEATH? That is exactly what the Bible says. Because of our sin, we literally earn death. God warned Adam in the garden that if he disobeyed the Lord, he would die (Gen. 2:17). There are two truths that every person has in common. We are all sinners, and we are all going to die someday. But God offers the free gift of eternal life through His Son, Jesus. This is the good news. Not many gifts I have given my wife have more value than the center diamond on her engagement ring. Michael, I want you to pretend my Bible here is a giant one-trillion-dollar diamond. Pretty large stone, isn't it? Could you purchase this from me?

I don't have that kind of cash on me at the moment. Ha!

What if you went to your immediate family, and all of you liquidated your combined resources? How about then? Could you purchase this diamond?

Nope. We wouldn't even come close.

Okay, I have another idea. Take all your family has and combine it with all the people in this restaurant. Every paying customer along with each employee. And top that off even further with each of their immediate family members' wealth and resources. Now we are talking about hundreds of people. If everyone combined every penny they earned for the rest of their lives, could you purchase the diamond from me then?

No. Still nowhere near one trillion dollars.

It seems impossible, but there is one way you could (Legally, stealing is not an option.) get this rare, incredibly expensive diamond from me. Do you know how?

I can't wait to find out.

I could give it to you, as a gift. Totally free. No strings attached. But you do have to RECEIVE it. You have to ACCEPT my gift. When I was a child, my parents mastered making Christmas morning the year's most special event. All of our family's gifts probably could have come close to being able to cram under the tree. But my parents spaced them out across the large family room and even overflowed them into adjacent rooms of our home. It appeared that we had a house full of presents. We could have each located the gifts intended only for us and simultaneously opened them rather quickly. Instead, we would observe patiently as only one family member was permitted to open a single gift at a time. The extended hours spent increased the excitement of the celebration for us as children. After the smaller gifts had been unwrapped, we would finally make it to the "grand finale."

Well after getting our new socks and underwear, each of us would receive the largest gift our parents knew would be most precious to us personally. When it was finally my turn, my parents would slide the giant package into the center of the room and say, "Merry Christmas, Josh. This is for you!"

I never once responded, "No thanks. I have been blessed enough. I am good with just my socks. Give it to one of my siblings." Yah right! I wasted no time jumping on top of that box, tearing the ribbon off with my teeth, and aggressively tossing the wrappings in every direction. I wasn't one to save the paper. Without question, there were Christmases I did not deserve my parents' good gifts. But whether or not I deserved them, I never let them down in how well I received them with joy. I don't understand how people all over the world who are hurting through the brokenness life can bring because of sin can hear the good news of the Gospel and essentially say "no thanks" as they reject Jesus' free gift of eternal life.

I get what you are saying. I have never really thought about any of this quite like this before.

A Savior Broken For You

Michael, here is something else to think about. True Christianity, faith in what the Bible teaches, is so different from every other religion in the world. All other faith systems can be categorized together in that you have to accomplish something(s) to earn your way to whatever it is they call their eternity. Christianity categorizes alone, in that it is not what you have done or what you can do, but rather what has already been done for you by Jesus, to provide a way to live forever with Him in a real place the Bible calls Heaven. What makes Heaven Heaven is not the absence of sin, sadness, tears, pain, or death (Rev. 21:4). It is not even the streets of gold (Rev. 21:21). (The best we have here on this Earth is the DIRT in Heaven.) What makes Heaven Heaven is that you are forever with Jesus.

As a practical thinker, I should recognize the uniqueness of Christianity. Michael, we should notice that it "stands out from the crowd." Listen, you cannot go to church enough, give to the offering plate enough, read your Bible enough, pray enough, or do enough "good things." You cannot crash airplanes into buildings, killing thousands. Faith in the Son of God, trusting Jesus as your personal Lord and Savior, is the only way to fix the broken relationship we have with God. It is the only way to be rescued from the punishment of our brokenness and escape an eternal death separated from the Lord in a real place the Bible calls Hell. What makes Hell Hell is not the presence of complete darkness, the lake of fire, or eternal anguish. (The never-ending pain, eternal death, literally causing your teeth to BANG against themselves (Matt. 13:42).)

What makes Hell Hell is that you are forever separated from Christ. The only way to Heaven is through Jesus.

> *For God so loved the world, that he gave his only Son, that whoever believes in him should not perish but have eternal life. (John 3:16 ESV)*

God SO loved MICHAEL, that He gave His only Son, that if MICHAEL believes in Him (MICHAEL) should not perish but have eternal life. I never believed in love at first sight. I love my wife more than anyone or anything apart from Jesus. But I didn't love her the first time I saw her. It took time to grow in our relationship with each other. We spent that time praying and seeking the Lord, waiting on Him to make it clear that we were to be married and spend the rest of our lives together. Love did not happen instantaneously for us. But ten and a half years ago, as I drove my wife to the hospital, and my HERO delivered my oldest son, Connor, I changed my mind when it came to love at first sight.

Without having spent any time together, creating memories, or having conversations, I loved my son the moment I laid eyes on him. This happened with all four of my children. My heart instantly bonded with theirs. If you tried to hurt my kids, I was coming after you. The moment each of them was born, I was willing to lay my life down for them, and I did not even "know" them yet. But God laid down His Son's life for me and for you, to take all our brokenness upon Himself (Luke 22:19). Our wickedness, our sin. As I have shared my faith with others, I have frequently been asked, "If God is a God of love, why would He let anyone go to Hell?"

My response has always been, "Why would He let anyone into His Heaven?" I don't understand that kind of love, but I am so incredibly thankful for it.

> *For by grace you have been saved through faith. And this is not your own doing; it is the gift of God, not a result of works, so that no one may boast. (Eph. 2:8–9 ESV)*

Michael, salvation comes by grace alone, through faith alone, through the shed blood of Jesus Christ alone. Mercy is God not giving us something we do deserve. Grace, on the other hand, is God giving us something we do not deserve. When you place your faith and trust in Jesus as your personal Lord and Savior, your relationship with God is restored. No longer broken. In that moment, God then sees you through "blood-stained glasses." By His grace, you receive the right to become a child of God (John 1:12). Forever a citizen of Heaven and joint heir of His Kingdom. No one will get to Heaven and scream at the top of their lungs, "Hey! I got here. I made it!" No one will boast about how incredible they were in life and how deserving they are of eternity in Heaven. I am saved, and the only thing I will boast about when I get to Heaven is Jesus and Him crucified (1 Cor. 2:2).

Jesus said to him, "I am the way, and the truth, and the life. No one comes to the Father except through me."
(John 14:6 ESV)

Jesus didn't say I am A way or I am a POSSIBLE way. He said, I am THE way. I hope to live a long, prosperous, and meaningful life. When I die, I pray it is at a ripe, old age and that it happens peacefully in my sleep. If it has to happen, wouldn't that be the best way to go? The reality is, tomorrow is not guaranteed for any of us. We could leave here after our lunch together, and I could get into a severe car accident on my way home. If you were to die today and if you stood before God and He asked you, "Michael, why should I let you into my Heaven?" What would you say?

Wow! I honestly don't know. What would you say?

Broken No More

I will tell you what I would not say. I wouldn't try to impress God with who I am or even all I have done for Him. Even as a pastor in local church ministry, I certainly would not profess to be a good person, worthy in any way of earning some right to enter Heaven. The Bible tells us that many will try to do just that, but God will cast them away because He never knew them (Matt. 7:22-23). My answer would be simple, "At the age of twelve years old, I understood my sin and my need for a Savior. I placed my faith and trust in Jesus Christ and in Him alone as the Son of God, the promised Savior of the world. I repented of my sin, turned away from it, and turned my heart toward Jesus. I asked the Lord to forgive me. I believe He died on the cross for me, in my place, conquered death, and rose from the grave. I received His free gift of salvation as I turned my life over to Him. In that moment, I was saved and became a child of God. Heaven is my home."

Why is it that the Bible remains the number one seller in the history of written literature? Why do the authors of the Gospels transparently record their mistakes rather than make themselves the heroes of their own stories? Why would they allow women in that culture to give first testimony of His resurrection in their written accounts, unless they were truly first to discover it? (Luke 24:1–12) How can any other explanation of Christ's empty tomb carry weight, when the Roman and religious leaders of that day went to such great lengths to eliminate all options of any claim other than Christ's resurrection? (Matt. 27:62–66)

True Christianity (the teachings of the Bible) stands alone. Jesus stands alone. Friend, I cannot PROVE to you today that there is a God. I cannot arrange a face-to-face introduction where you can physically shake God's hand and say hello. I know He is real. I have a relationship with Him. God loves you. He wants you. He reveals Himself through His Word. He answers prayer. He has changed every aspect of my life, and it continues to be my honor to serve Him. There will always be a "faith element" in the "equation of salvation." When you sat down in your chair, you actively placed your faith in that piece of furniture, trusting it would sustain your weight. What I would like to know is, is there anything keeping you from placing your faith in Jesus right now?

No. No there isn't. I need Jesus now!

Michael, I would love to lead you in a prayer. The words I speak, the prayer itself, is not what saves you. It is kind of like when I got married. The pastor said, "Josh, say this to Erin." It was not the words he asked me to repeat, but whether or not I meant those words from my heart to hers that gave the words value. Pray this from your heart to God's heart.

Lord, Jesus.
Lord, Jesus.
I know that I am a sinner.
I know that I am a sinner.
And that is a problem. It keeps me from you.
And that is a problem. It keeps me from you.
I am sorry. Please forgive me. I turn away from
my sin, and I turn toward you, Lord.
I am sorry. Please forgive me. I turn away from
my sin, and I turn toward you, Lord.
I believe you are who you said you are. The
Son of God. The Savior of the world.
I believe you are who you said you are. The
Son of God. The Savior of the world.

And I believe you did what you said you did. You died on the cross for my sin, in my place, and three days later you miraculously rose from the grave!
And I believe you did what you said you did. You died on the cross for my sin, in my place, and three days later you miraculously rose from the grave!
I place my faith and trust in you and in you alone. I accept and receive your free gift of salvation.
I place my faith and trust in you and in you alone. I accept and receive your free gift of salvation.
Come into my life. Be Lord of my life. And help me to live for you for the rest of my life.
Come into my life. Be Lord of my life. And help me to live for you for the rest of my life.
In Jesus' name, AMEN.
In Jesus' name, AMEN.

What's Next?

Maybe you have never trusted Jesus as your personal Lord and Savior. Perhaps you have just read through this dialogue I had with Michael, and you have come to understand your need to surrender your life to Christ. The Bible says today is the day of salvation (*2 Cor. 6:2*). You too can pray that prayer from your heart to God's heart. You too can believe in the Lord Jesus Christ and be saved (*Acts 16:31*). Please, say yes to Jesus today.

If you *have* just made the decision to place your faith and trust in Jesus Christ as your personal Lord and Savior or if you still have questions about that decision and God's redemptive plan (found in His Word) for the brokenness in our lives, please feel free to contact me at jhales697@gmail.com. I want to know about (and rejoice with you over) your newfound relationship with Jesus. It would be my privilege to help you in any way I can on your spiritual journey.

There are three essential next steps for the new believer in Christ.

Quiet Time: Let me encourage you to get into God's Word. Devote daily time to develop this discipline in your life. A good place to start reading is in the Gospel of *John*, the fourth book of the New Testament. Study the life and ministry of your Savior. Grow in relationship with Him. Spend time daily on your knees in prayer, talking with the Lord. No conversation is off limits. Seek the face of God hard (*Psalm 27:8*).

Church: Get connected with other believers in a local church ministry that preaches the Word of God. The church is the body of Christ (*1 Cor. 12:27*), your family. This is where you can grow and mature in your understanding of Scripture as well as the Christian life. You need to be discipled. Have a spirit of invitation to other believers ready and available to pour into your life.

Baptism: Baptism is the next and first step for the new believer in Christ. Biblical baptism is full submersion, exemplified by Jesus when He was baptized by his cousin, *John* (*Matt. 3:13–17*). Baptism is in no way part of salvation. The thief crucified next to Jesus was saved in his final moments alive on Earth without any opportunity to be baptized (*Luke 23:42–43*). You are saved by God's grace through faith in His Son, Jesus. There is nothing magical about the water. You are not having your sins "washed off" of you.

Baptism is primarily an act of *obedience* to God (*Matthew 28*) that FOLLOWS salvation. If you are not saved, and you get baptized, you are just getting wet. Additionally, baptism is a *picture* of what Christ did for us. When you go under the water, it is a picture of Jesus' death and burial. When you come out of the water, it is a picture of His resurrection. (*Rom. 6:4*) When being baptized, you are "preaching" the Gospel without necessarily saying a single word. Lastly, baptism is a public testimony of your faith and *identity* in Christ. You are publicly "saying" *I am with Jesus, and I want you all to know.*

EXTRA SCENE

I had just turned twenty years old. I was still a teenager just a few months before. I hadn't "grown up" yet, and I still lacked the wisdom that comes with life's experiences. This was before drinking, before marriage, and before I was a father. This was before vocational ministry.

I was living on my own for the very first time. I managed an indoor soccer sportsplex, a pretty good gig for a young man. (That job provided experience that shaped many of the sports ministries I have directed over the years.) I had plans to visit a friend attending college faraway out of state. I arranged some time off in the staff schedule at work. I was excited for the weekend-long stay on campus, and I wanted to make our visit together as lengthy as possible. Traveling from northern Ohio all the way to Iowa, it seemed logical to me to start driving immediately after work late Friday night, with the intention to arrive back at work just in time for my Monday evening shift. Oh, to be young again. It was a projected ten-hour-long trip, interrupted by a dangerous Iowa blizzard that added nearly four hours to my travels. And that was just one way.

I left late into the night, following a ten-plus hour-long shift, after locking up midway through a tournament weekend. My car was packed. The gas tank was full, and I purchased a fast-food meal, ready to conquer the open, dark road. I had several caffeinated drinks on standby. That was the longest trip I had ever driven alone before. I was already yawning before I even pulled onto the highway.

Cell phones were not really a thing yet. GPS didn't even exist. I was completely dependent on my printed-out-map-quest directions. It was winter, but for some reason, I felt it was not an issue to be traveling in shorts and my work T-shirt. Why would I need pants or a coat? There was heat in the car. So many things could have gone wrong. I was not prepared for a single one of them.

The temperature continued to drop as I traveled through state lines, getting closer and closer to my destination. I learned one very specific difference between Ohio and Iowa (back then) that I had no clue about before that trip. I knew Ohio used salt on their highways to melt the ice. Iowa just lays down a layer of dirt or sand to give the roads a sense of grittiness, I suppose. I had traveled all through the night and watched the sun rise. I was struggling to keep my burning eyes open, with the radio blaring and the windows cracked to allow a jet stream of freezing cold air in to keep me awake. Vehicles traveling in the mid to high seventy-miles-per-hour range suddenly halted to a steady fifteen to twenty miles per hour. It was impossible to see the cars in front of me through the giant blowing snowflakes slamming against my windshield. As the driving speeds slowed even more drastically, I peeked out my side window to see the road covered in ice, inches thick. We were all driving on a "hockey rink."

Almost every mile marker it seemed, I saw vehicles broken down on the side of the road. Then, almost as if like a domino effect, semitrucks were flipped over in ditches, as well as even police cars. I knew this trip had become incredibly dangerous. For safety alone, I was tempted to pull off to the side of the road and wait out the blizzard. But with the increased vision impairment, that really was not an option. It could have proven to be even more dangerous. As I cruised along, traveling just above five miles per hour, doing my best not to "fishtail," I was committed to just keep going.

Anyone who knows me well will attest to just how uncomfortable I am driving on the ice. My extreme discomfort probably started with that Iowa trip. My wife may be the only person who really knows how uncomfortable I am driving next to semitrucks.

You trap me between a couple of those monster trailers in the midst of bad weather, and I am a mess.

I will give you one guess what happened next. Thankful for the incredibly slow speeds and unable to see through the snow, I found myself with a semitruck in front of me and one behind me, while driving between two others, both to my left and right. The four trucks had me boxed in. If the one in front suddenly stopped, I would slide forward and crash into it. The one behind me would certainly slide forward as well, squeezing my car like an accordion between the two. If either semitruck next to me couldn't see my car and attempted to change lanes, I was in trouble. Any number of scenarios could have turned my vehicle into a "ping-pong ball" bouncing back-and-forth between those mammoth trucks. As I strained to keep my fatigued eyes open, I just kept saying to myself, "Slow and steady, slow and steady."

I continued to progress forward with the other giant trucks surrounding me, when I lost all control of my tires on the ice. I started spinning in a circle, slowly at first. My rotation sped up like a top, still sliding straight forward, directly in the center of those semitrailers. I felt like a kid on the park merry-go-round, begging the bully to stop spinning it so fast. I cried out to God, "Lord, save me!" As one of the side trucks pulled forward in "slow motion," I began to veer toward its back end. I just missed smacking into it by inches, as I slid off the road and into a ditch, like a spinning coin finding the edge of the table.

My car's front end was facing down into the deep ditch. The automobile was front-wheel drive, with the weight of the engine "cementing" the tires into the slushy, muddy snowbank. As far as I could tell, there was nothing broken about the car itself. Just the predicament I was in. The good news was, I was completely off the road. The bad news was, I was wearing shorts and a T-shirt. I had no coat, and the heat of the car was going to run out soon because my gas tank was nearing empty. I had no idea where I was at, and walking for help likely meant freezing to death, if not being hit by another vehicle. There was no chance I was getting out of this on my own.

There was nothing I could do but ask God for help. I closed my tired eyes and laid my forehead on the steering wheel. "Lord, I am in real danger right now. I have zero options. I need you to rescue me." As I spoke the word "amen," closing out that desperate prayer, I opened my eyes to the sound of a key tapping on the driver's side window. Outside my car, in the "frozen tundra," was the oddest thing I had ever seen. There was an unshaven man, wearing a cowboy hat, work boots, ripped jeans barely held together, a skin-tight (stained) tank top, with a piece of straw hanging out of his mouth. The weather seemed to not affect him at all, as if it was a warm summer day. I still don't have a clue where he got a piece of straw. Behind him was an old dented pickup truck, with a rusted-out bed, and duct tape literally holding pieces of it in place.

I put down my window a few inches, and with the thickest southern accent, he said, "Do ya need a tow?"

Surprised and confused, I responded with gratitude, "Yes, please!"

Trudging through the snow, he dropped his broken tailgate, to unveil the shiniest, newest-looking cable pulley system. It looked like it was made of diamonds. None of what occurred that day made sense to me. I still cannot explain any of it. That "good Samaritan" attached his crystal-like cable to the rear frame under my car, rolling around in the piles of snow, with not a red mark on any of his bare skin to indicate at all just how cold he should have been. He said with his thick accent, "Now, when I hollar go, you pop it in reverse." I agreed. He pulled me from that ditch effortlessly. In the excitement of being rescued and able to get back on the road again, I turned my face out the window to thank him. But he and his truck were gone before I even had a chance. God had answered my prayer, and I could not explain what had just taken place.

I was exhausted. I needed to sleep badly. I am not sure I have ever been that tired again in my life. My mind was "fried." I will never claim that that experience was anything supernatural. But when I arrived on campus in one piece and could get to a phone, Mom and I joked that my guardian angel is a hillbilly. I do wonder at times, when I get to Heaven, if I will meet that man again.

I don't know what struggles you are going through right now. I don't know if you are "driving cautiously on the ice," surrounded by the pressures of life closing in on you. I don't know if you are "stuck in a ditch," feeling all hope is lost, needing to be saved. What I do know is that we all have our own stories, complete with broken pieces the Lord would love to repurpose. There is nothing you can go through that God is unaware of. There is nothing outside of His control.

Seek after the Lord, when sin is breaking you down. Seek after the Lord in your relationships. Seek after the Lord when nothing makes sense and you are ready to give up. Seek after the Lord when life is unfair. Seek after the Lord when it is hard to trust. Seek after the Lord for eternal security. Seek after the Lord, and He will reveal Himself to you. Seek after the Lord, His Kingdom and His righteousness, and He *will* make sense of all your brokenness (*Matt. 6:33*).

God loves you. He wants you. And He has a plan for your life. When you feel *broken* and *unusable*, there is no better place to be than in the presence of the Lord. When all you have left is to cry out to Him, do it. When there is nowhere else to turn except to the pages of Scripture, do that too. When you feel you can no longer stand, but nothing in you wants to fall to your knees, do it anyway. Nothing takes Him by surprise, and God is more than capable of providing rescue in your time of need. If He chooses not to, trust that He will use your circumstances to help someone else in their broken time.

I don't know what God has chosen to do with this book. I am going to let Him figure that part out. If the time and energy spent to write it was for no other reason than for me to personally be reminded of His goodness, faithfulness, and call on my life, then that time and energy has not been wasted. If this book helps just one person, then it has all been worth it. I have meditated on these pages, and I pray that I have worshiped the Lord in writing them. I have experienced the presence of God during this project, uniquely from any other time in my life and ministry.

I wrote this book for my children. I know they will someday read it, and I hope they will pass it down to their children and grandchildren as well. In a world that seems more broken than it has ever been before, my family will hear many voices and messages not in agreement with the Word of God. Long after I have left this life, I hope to be a voice that continues to point them (and others) to Jesus. The biblical principles and timeless truths written within these pages, along with the life lessons I have learned along the way, are of greatest value for me to pass down to my kids.

I want to thank you again for taking the time to read this book. I hope the stories I have told of my journey have resonated with your own. I pray the real-life accounts in Scripture tied to the messages I have shared here are a blessing to you as well. Mostly, I hope you have come to fully understand that we are all **BROKEN BUT STILL USABLE.**

For His glory, to advance His Kingdom,
Pastor Joshua A. Hales

About the Author

PASTOR JOSHUA A. HALES is a leader in both the student and worship ministries at the church he is currently a member of near Dayton, Ohio. In addition to formal studies through Chicago's Moody Bible Institute, Josh was licensed to preach in 2007 and ordained in the Gospel ministry in 2017. Josh has over twenty years of experience in student and camp ministries. Josh is passionate about the local church and impacting surrounding communities, doing whatever it takes to get as many as possible in front of the Gospel of Jesus Christ. He and his wife, Erin, serve together and have four children. Authoring ***BROKEN BUT STILL USABLE… just like me*** has been an incredible unforeseen experience. Pastor Josh never would have guessed there was a book inside him, and it all started over two decades ago with this life-altering verse.

The end of the matter; all has been heard.
Fear God and keep his commandments, for this is
the whole duty of man. (Ecc. 12:13 ESV)